The Princeton Review

Job Notes:
Interviews

The Princeton Review

Job Notes:
Interviews

BY MARCI TAUB

Random House, Inc.
New York 1997
http://www.randomhouse.com

Princeton Review Publishing, L.L.C.
2315 Broadway, 2nd Floor
New York, NY 10024
e-mail: info@review.com

ISBN 0-679-77875-6

Editor: Amy E. Zavatto
Designer: Illeny Maaza
Production Editor: Bruno Blumenfeld

Manufactured in the United States of America on partially recycled paper.

9 8 7 6 5 4 3 2 1

First Edition

DEDICATION

For my beloved husband Adam. His friendship, advice, humor, and patience helped make this book possible. And for our daughter, Kyra. It's about feeling good about who you are, standing up for what you believe in, and going after what you want.

ACKNOWLEDGMENTS

Special thanks to Amy Zavatto, my editor, who has contributed her insight, collegiality, and professionalism to this project. I am grateful to both my clients and students. It is a privilege to work with diverse and spirited people who pose new strategic challenges during every session and class.

My deepest appreciation goes to my sister Ellyn Karetnick for being a kindred spirit. Thank you to my friends Andrea Meyer, Elissa Tomasetti, and Michelle Weichert for the profound difference they make in my life. My mother, Arlene Karetnick, has always been there for me. She is a remarkable mother, friend, and individual. A heartfelt thanks to Cheryl and Mel Taub who have always lent a hand, an ear, and a word of encouragement.

Contents

Introduction

Do you picture a job interview like a secret police interrogation in some political action thriller? An interviewer, alias "Interrogator," leads you to a secluded conference room. The door closes behind you with a resounding thud and you are led to a straight-backed wooden chair. The interviewer paces the room, firing question after question that seem impossible to answer without incriminating yourself. You hear yourself answering in a strange, disembodied voice—confessing to hating your last boss, revealing that your greatest weakness is your inability to deal with authority figures, and rambling incoherently in response to: "Tell me a little about yourself." Beads of sweat form on your upper lip and trickle down the sides of your temples. At the same time, your hands begin to feel cold and clammy and your stomach feels like bats are flying around in it. You wonder if you're going to pass out on the spot and wake up to realize it was all only a bad dream.

Most of us approach the interviewing process fearing this type of scenario. And some of us can tell real life stories about an interview-from-hell. The way to transform an interview from an endurance test into a no-brainer is to remember that it's a chance for both you and the interviewer to get to know each other. Like a blind date, you can check each other out to see if you're compatible. So relax, ask the interviewer thoughtful questions, and be an active listener. You don't need to stress yourself out trying to impress the interviewer or spend all of your time and energy focusing on getting them to like you. If you do, you won't have a chance to notice if you like the position, organizational culture, and interviewer's style. And you'll come across as overeager at best, or desperate at worst.

You've already worked so hard in your job search to get to the interviewing stage. Networking, writing cover letters, and preparing resumes have enabled you to get your foot in the door of an organization. Now, in an interview, you'll have the chance to sell yourself in person and to check out the job and organization more thoroughly. The good news is that there are innovative, easy strategies that you can use as an entry-level or young professional to prepare for, maximize, and successfully follow-up an interview.

In the chapters that follow you'll learn advanced strategies that are usually known only to more experienced professionals. Through vignettes based on real job candidates' experiences, you'll discover tactics for approaching the interviewing process. Then you'll learn strategies presented both as step-by-step methods and responses to frequently asked questions (FAQs) about the three phases of the interviewing process: before, during, and after. You'll also have the chance to practice and organize these strategies as you progress through the interviewing phase of your job search. Examples and worksheets throughout the chapters will help you turn any interview into a job lander.

Before the Interview —Package Yourself

STEP 1: TRACK THE SMALL STUFF

Kristin finally gets invited to interview for her dream job. When the call comes to schedule the interview, she's so excited that she jots down the information on a scrap of paper, thanks the caller, and immediately phones her best friend with the good news. Her friend, Will, congratulates her and asks her a few basic questions about the interview. Will wants to know when it is. Kristin looks down at her scribbled notes and replies, "It's on the second at 3:00 P.M.. Or, uh . . . er . . . maybe it's on the third at 2:00 P.M. I can't quite make out my writing—it says 2 @ 3. Oh, no, what am I going to do?"

Will then reminds Kristin that she has another interview scheduled for 11:00 A.M. that day and wonders what happens if it's a long one. She realizes suddenly that she hasn't left herself any extra time in case the interviewer wants her to meet other employees or is running late.

How many interviews should I schedule in one day?

Only schedule as many as you can reasonably handle. Don't compare yourself with others. Depending on your personal schedule, commute time, and energy level, you can arrange as few or as many as you want. One advantage of scheduling multiple interviews for the same day is that you'll be in the interview zone. That is, you'll be dressed appropriately and in the mindset to interview. So you're more likely to get on a roll and have a good day.

For the crowning blow, Will asks who she's meeting with and where the office is located. Finally, Kristin thinks to herself, she's got something straight. Then she discovers that she only wrote down the person's last name and has no idea if it's a man or a woman. *And* she recorded an incomplete address— Greenwich could mean Greenwich Street or Greenwich Avenue.

Some of these mistakes are more easily remedied than others. But even so, having to do double work is a waste of your valuable time and could cast you in a negative light. So save yourself a lot of trouble up front by carefully recording all information pertaining to your interview in your appointment book or organizer, or at least transferring it there immediately after you hang up the phone. While you're on the phone, listen carefully, ask for clarification if you're not sure of something, and summarize what was said to you as a way to end the conversation. For example, "Thank you for your call. I'm looking forward to meeting with Ms. Smith at 8:30 A.M. on Tuesday, November 24th at XYZ Tower Square, Suite 614."

STEP 2: DO YOUR HOMEWORK

There Michael is in the interviewer's office. He feels confident that he can wing it and get by on his charisma and general knowledge of the work world. The interviewer's first question is, "What do you know about our company?" Michael stares blankly, his jaw drops, and he fumbles to come up with something to say that will sound semi-intelligent. Finally, he says something vague and irrelevant: "Everyone knows that it's a great company and I want to be a part of it too." The interviewer asks him one more brief question, extends his hand, and thanks Michael for stopping by. His interview is over in under ten minutes and his chance at getting the job is gone.

How can I schedule interviews if I'm working full-time? FAQ

It can be tough to find the time and privacy to make a phone call to a prospective employer. Be creative. Borrow a colleague's office if you don't have one. Just make sure you don't keep disappearing behind closed doors more frequently than usual or you'll look suspicious.

Or find a pay phone nearby on your lunch hour and use a calling card. Never use coins in a pay phone. The impression you make shouldn't include the background noise of coins dropping and an operator's recorded voice droning, "Please insert 30 cents . . . " The employer will undoubtedly question your judgment and professionalism as you fumble to insert change in the phone or have to call them back because you got cut off.

Another solution is to speak with a prospective employer either at the beginning or end of the day. Sometimes just getting to work early or staying late can give you the privacy you need.

This story is an all too common one. Recruiters and hiring managers are continually amazed that otherwise qualified candidates have the audacity and lack of common sense to arrive at an interview so unprepared. And the ironic thing is that such clueless candidates as Michael make those candidates who are even minimally prepared look even better to prospective employers. A little prep goes a long way.

To really prepare for interview you need to research four things: your career field, the position, the organization, and general current events. Your ability to speak clearly about trends in your field will show that you're committed to growth and excited about the field. Your working knowledge of the position will enable you to correlate your skills with the employer's needs. Your research about the organization's history, status in the industry, and future direction will reveal to the interviewer your genuine interest in working for her organization. Your knowledge of current events in the world will prove to the employer that you are a curious, well-informed professional who keeps on top of the latest happenings which may impact your profession.

What if the interviewer suggests a date and/or time that is inconvenient for me?

Don't be afraid to tell the interviewer if the time and/or date suggested conflicts with another interview or with mandatory work or a personal commitment. Politely and briefly explain that you are unable to interview then. Always be prepared to suggest alternate times and/or dates right away to demonstrate your willingness to interview and your flexibility. In this case, it's particularly important to reinforce your interest in the position so the interviewer doesn't think you're brushing her off.

You can research all of this information by reading and talking with people. Read career guidebooks, company directories with profiles, government publications, popular newspapers and magazines, and trade and professional association publications. These kinds of resources are easily accessible in many different places, including career center libraries, public libraries, college and university libraries, bookstores, newsstands, and on the Internet. Beware, though, that printed material becomes outdated very quickly. Some types of information generally have a longer shelf life than others. For example, written information about your career field and the position you're interested in will probably remain stable longer than data about the organization and general current events. There's nothing more embarrassing than going into an interview and confidently referring to the wrong CEO, not knowing about a huge merger between two key organizations in the industry, or calling your field position by an outdated name. So stay on top of recent developments in all of these areas in order to keep your foot out of your mouth.

Resources for researching fields and occupations

ABI/Inform—CD-ROM database, which indexes and abstracts articles from more than 800 business and trade journals over the past five years.

Dictionary of Occupational Titles—U.S. Department of Labor. Most recently updated in 1991, this resource is a bit cumbersome, but it provides some useful information regarding the specific tasks performed on each of the 12,741 jobs listed.

Encyclopedia of Associations—Gale Research, Inc., Detroit, MI, 1996. Lists over 25,000 associations, clubs, and other nonprofit groups. These organizations and their members are often excellent sources of information about a given field. Some may have local chapters in your region, and many offer reduced membership rates for students and recent graduates.

Job Hunter's Sourcebook—Gale Research, Inc., Detroit, MI, 1996. Provides a comprehensive listing of information sources for 155 popular occupations.

Jobs '96—Kathryn Petras and Ross Petras. Fireside, New York, 1995. Numerous descriptions of jobs in various industries. Includes average salaries, hiring qualifications, and current job, industry, and regional employment trends. Highlights careers that have the best long-term potential.

National Trade and Professional Associations of the United States—Columbia Books, Inc., Washington, D.C. Information on over 7,000 associations including: history and purpose, when and where they meet, what they publish, and the names of key contacts.

Newsletters in Print—Gale Research, Inc., Detroit, MI, 1995. Lists over 10,000 newsletters on a variety of subjects.

Newspaper Abstracts (CD-ROM)—Indexes articles from such major newspapers as *The New York Times*, *Wall Street Journal*, *Washington Post*, and *Los Angeles Times*.

The Occupational Outlook Handbook—U.S. Department of Labor. Updated every two years. Offers a broad overview of over 250 occupations, which account for nearly 85 percent of the labor force.

Periodical Abstracts—This CD-ROM indexes and abstracts over 2,000 popular and scholarly periodicals.

Predicasts F&S Index U.S.—CD-ROM includes citations, abstracts, and complete text of articles from over 1,000 business and trade publications.

Professional Careers Sourcebook—Gale Research, Inc., Detroit, MI, 1995. Information on 118 high profile occupations, job descriptions, lists of career guides, professional associations, trade journals, and industry conventions.

Regional, State, and Local Organizations—Gale Research, Inc., Detroit, MI, 1995. Similar to the *Encyclopedia of Associations* except that the more than 50,000 organizations listed are at the local, state, or regional level.

Standard and Poors Industry Surveys—Provides general information and financial forecasts for 25 industrial groups.

How much time should I allow for an interview?

When you arrange or confirm an interview, it's okay to ask approximately how long you can expect to be there. Even so, be prepared for the possibility that an employer may want you to meet, informally or formally, with some of their colleagues. This is especially true if you hit it off with your interviewer. That's why it's important to leave extra time in your schedule for an interview if possible. If not, when an interviewer asks you if you can stay to meet others, you can say that you regrettably can't. But that you're happy to come back at your mutual earliest convenience.

Resources for researching organizations

ABI/Inform—CD-ROM database that indexes and abstracts articles from more than 800 business and trade journals over the past five years.

Annual Reports—Available at many libraries, campus career centers or by calling the organization directly. Includes information on the company's financial performance and other aspects of operation.

Better Business Bureau—If you're researching a local company the BBB may be able to tell you how many complaints have been lodged against the firm. Ironically, some BBB offices charge fees to provide this information.

Business Periodicals Index—This CD-ROM indexes roughly 350 periodicals covering all business fields.

Chambers of Commerce—One of the best sources of information on smaller local companies. Look in the *World Chamber of Commerce Directory* to find the Chamber of Commerce for the region you are investigating.

Cracking the Corporate Closet: The 200 Best (and worst) Companies to Work for, Buy from, and Invest in If You're Gay or Lesbian—and Even if You Aren't—Daniel B. Baker, Sean O'Brien Strub, and Bill Henning. Harper Collins, New York, 1995.

Disclosure/Worldscope—This CD-ROM provides information abstracted from reports filed with the SEC on over 12,000 public companies.

Infotrac (General Business File)—CD-ROM database that indexes and abstracts articles from more than 800 business, economic management and trade journals, and newspapers from the past two years.

The Job Seeker's Guide to Socially Responsible Companies—Katherine Jankowski. 1994. Describes nearly 1,000 companies that have distinguished themselves by being socially conscious. Includes information on job application procedures.

Moody's Manuals—For companies listed on U.S. stock exchanges, provides information on company history, products, and financials.

Newspaper Abstracts (CD-ROM)—Indexes articles in such major U.S. newspapers as *The New York Times*, *Wall Street Journal*, *Washington Post*, and *Los Angeles Times*.

The 100 Best Companies for Gay Men and Lesbians—Ed Mickens. Pocket Books: New York, 1994.

Periodical Abstracts—This CD-ROM indexes and abstracts over 2,000 popular and scholarly periodicals.

Predicasts F&S Index U.S.—CD-ROM includes citations, abstracts, and complete text of articles from over 1,000 business and trade publications. Indexed by SIC codes.

Shopping for a Better World—Council on Economic Priorities. This handy guide rates approximately 200 employers in a variety of categories including charitable giving, advancement of women and minorities, family benefits, and environmental policies.

Standard and Poor's Corporation Records—Offers profiles of publicly held American companies, in addition to providing financial data.

10K Reports—Public companies must submit these to the Securities and Exchange Commission. One section of this report lets you know if any legal proceedings have been brought against the company.

How much should I know about my career field or industry as a whole?

You should know enough to discuss clearly: (1) your short and long-term career goals; (2) what in your background contributed to these goals and has prepared you for the position you're interviewing for; and (3) some current trends or issues related to the field or industry which have been prominent in the news lately.

Talk to anyone and everyone who knows about your field, position, organization and current events of interest. Transfer the key information you discover through both reading and talking to interview cheat sheets. You can use these sheets to prepare for interviews and even bring them with you for quick reference before or in between interviews.

Sample Interview Cheat Sheet

About the Organization

Organization Name:	Written Word Publishers, Inc.
Position Available:	Editorial Assistant
Department:	Children's Books
Address:	682 Quotation Street
	New York, NY 11111
	Human Resources dept. is on 18th floor Mr. Italics, Human Resources Manager, ext. 444. Remember to get first name for thank-you note.
Phone #:	111-1112
Fax #:	212-222-2222
E-mail:	Ask for at interview
Interview Date:	Will be finalized 2/17
Number of Employees:	125
Year Organization Founded:	1946
Locations of Offices:	NY (headquarters) and L.A.
Relevant Financial Status:	Highest profits ever in 1995 after decline in late '80s and early '90s. Growth due to expansion of trade paperback division.
Key Managers/Principals:	CEO is Mr. George Parentheses (blueblood type; co-founded by his father; will be retiring at end of this year). Mr. P's thirtysomething grandson George Parentheses III just became Editor-in Chief.
Products/Services:	All major book publishing divisions except textbooks.
New Directions:	Children's Books Department growing. Heavily involved in educational multimedia.
Organizational Culture:	Changed from conservative to more progressive and risk-taking due to grandson's influence.

Ways to Get Brownie Points

Media Coverage:	Mention articles in *Time, The New York Times,* and *The Washington Post* last summer about change of leadership and new directions. Article last month in *Publisher's Weekly* on new CD-ROM. Profile in *Forbes* on George III last January.
Flattery:	Mention CD-ROM I tried out. Great graphics, innovative educational approach. My contact at Women in Communications said Written Word has the most respected children's books in the industry.
Inside Info:	Jane (former Written Word intern I met at conference) said they like excellent computer skills—also like experience with children. Remember to mention the nanny job that's not on my resume.
Questions I Can Ask:	How will the new direction into educational multimedia affect day-to-day operations and staffing? Is the person who last filled this position still with the company?

You don't need to know every statistic from the organization's annual report—but you do need to show that you know why you're there, what you're getting into, and how it all fits together with what's going on in the world. So do your homework about each organization you're going to interview at and you'll set yourself apart from the many unprepared candidates you're competing with for the job.

What if the interview comes up suddenly and I have only a day to do my research?

Ideally, you should try to schedule the interview at least a couple of days ahead so that you have ample time to do your homework. If, for some reason, you must interview on short notice, do the best you can. A quick trip to the library, a scan of Internet resources, and a brief conversation with a few key people who know about the organization and/or industry can help you ace the interview.

Step 3: Dress for Success

Sitting in the reception area of a progressive graphic design firm, employees stream by Marissa wearing neon-colored, trendy clothing. She feels uncomfortable and out of place dressed in her most conservative, navy pin-striped suit. Glancing furtively at her watch, Marissa wonders if she has time to slip out the door and run home four blocks to change before her interview. She self-consciously tries to hide behind her large, leather portfolio. When the interviewer—wearing trendy but professional clothes—approaches Marissa, she resists the urge to dive behind the sofa out of sheer embarrassment.

That night she compared notes with her job-searching roommate, Susan. Susan consoled Marissa by relaying the opposite scenario from her day. Susan had interviewed at a small, conservative management consulting firm wearing a sporty pantsuit. Both of them realized that they made common, but potentially interview-blowing errors.

There are so many different kinds of dress codes across industries that it's impossible to generalize about the perfect interview outfit for every situation. The rule of thumb is to ask yourself, "What do people in that job at that type of organization wear every day on the job?" Then go one level up in conservatism and formality. There *are* a few general "no ways":

- No messy stuff. Neatness counts, it shows that you have pride in yourself and that you care about the interview.

- No uncomfortable stuff. Tugging at a tight-waisted skirt or a too stiff button-down shirt will make you preoccupied with what you're wearing instead of what's going on in the interview.

- No complicated stuff. Unless you're interviewing with a fashion designer, keep it simple.

- No overwhelming cologne or perfume, conspicuous jewelry, or overstated clothes.

STEP 4: DEFINE YOUR SKILLS PROFILE

In Andrew's interview from hell, an employer asked him right away, "What are your strengths?" He replied, "Well, lots of things. Like, um well, once I did some writing. And another time I used the computer a little. Last year I helped some people learn some new research methods."Andrew went on for about five minutes, giving the interviewer a generalized, jumbled list of skills. During his struggling recitation, the interviewer's eyes started to glaze over and he began drumming the fingers of his left hand on the desk.

What should I wear to an interview if it's on a Casual Friday?

Even on a Casual Day don't dress casually. Remember that you're still going to an interview. As always, the unacceptable casual extremes are obvious: no jeans (ripped or not) and no Hawaiian shirts, for starters. Ask your friends and contacts in the field for advice on the typical going look on a regular day and then wear something a little nicer than what they say. You need to show respect for the fact that you're a guest at an organization and that you're there to discuss business, not just blend in with the crowd.

Oblivious, Andrew finally came up for air and the interviewer rephrased the question in a more direct way, as, "Why are you qualified for *this* position?" Andrew looked at him, confused, and started mumbling about how he could do all of the things he just mentioned. When Andrew started to struggle to come up with something again, the interviewer cut him off.

"What one thing would your last boss say about you?" he asked. Startled, Andrew couldn't figure out what he was doing wrong. He finally came up with, "She would say I was a quick learner." The interviewer responded, "That's it?" Needless to say, the interviewer was unimpressed by Andrew's limited answer, which it had taken three tries to elicit from nim. The interview continued downhill from there and ended shortly thereafter.

When an interviewer wants to know what you've got to offer as a potential employee, you're expected to be able to articulate your specific, related skills. And, as you'll learn in Steps 5 and 6, that's just the beginning. In Andrew's case, instead of just calling himself a quick learner, he could have added some skills to back up just what it was he's learned, such as writing reports, researching, organizing projects, analyzing spreadsheets, performing word processing functions, working well with others, training new employees, and leading meetings.

You need to define your strengths, or skills package before you get to the interview. The easy way to do this is to think of your skills as falling into three categories: *I am*, *I can*, and *I know*. The *I am* skills are the broadest ones in that they reflect your capabilities, talents, and general areas of strength. They even border on personality characteristics. For example, you might say, "I am artistic; I am mechanically-inclined; I am easy-going; and I am detail-oriented." The skills in this category are highly versatile and can be valued in any number of career fields.

The *I can* skills are next broadest but are a little more specifically linked to activities. They are such things as "I can speak French fluently; I can do word processing; and I can balance a budget." The *I can* skills are also transferable among many different fields.

The *I know* skills are the most narrowly defined and most closely connected to a particular activity or content area. They might be, for example, "I know French business vocabulary; I know Microsoft Word; and I can monitor accounts payable and receivable in a retail business." Think of these skills as different fields of knowledge you may have.

The following checklists will guide you in targeting your skills in each of these categories. You'll probably be pleasantly surprised at how many skills you have that you didn't even realize were marketable.

The *I Am* Skills

Read the following list of skills and check off the ones that sound like you. Don't think too hard about each skill, go more with your gut reaction. I am…

adaptable	____	loyal	____
analytical	____	mechanically-inclined	____
artistic	____	musically-inclined	____
assertive	____	numerically-inclined	____
athletic	____	observant	____
calm	____	open-minded	____
cheerful	____	outgoing	____
confident	____	organized	____
congenial	____	patient	____
conscientious	____	perceptive	____
cooperative	____	persevering	____
creative	____	persuasive	____
curious	____	poised	____
dependable	____	practical	____
detail-oriented	____	punctual	____
disciplined	____	quiet	____
diplomatic	____	realistic	____
discreet	____	reserved	____
efficient	____	resourceful	____
energetic	____	responsible	____
enterprising	____	scholarly	____
enthusiastic	____	sensitive	____
expressive	____	serious	____
flexible	____	sincere	____
funny	____	tactful	____
good with languages	____	team-oriented	____
honest	____	technically-inclined	____
idealistic	____	thoughtful	____
independent	____	visionary	____
industrious	____		
inventive	____		

After checking off the characteristics that describe you, go back and circle the six words that BEST describe you. Write these in the *I Am* section of the Skills Profile that follows on page 19.

One way to find out if you're making an accurate assessment of your *I Am* skills is to have someone who knows you well (parent, partner or friend) review your list. Have this person review your lists. Sometimes others can have insightful comments or can identify skills you didn't even know you had.

What if I don't have many skills?

It's okay if you believe you only do a couple of things well. Focus on them and how they relate to your prospective job. Then show the interviewer how you can use these skills to immediately add value to her organization. It's better to shine in a couple of well-defined areas which are integral to the position you're applying for then to try to come off as a Renaissance man or woman. Unless, of course, you're really a Leonardo da Vinci type and can demonstrate your abilities in a broad range of relevant areas.

The *I Can* Skills

Check off the things you can do or that you think you have the potential to develop. Don't worry about your level of proficiency. Remember, you're being hired as much for your potential as for your acquired skills.

	Can Do Now	Could Develop
advise or counsel others	____	____
analyze quantitative data	____	____
analyze situations or problems	____	____
appraise values	____	____
assess needs	____	____
brainstorm ideas	____	____
budget	____	____
calculate/compute numbers with ease	____	____
care for animals	____	____
care for children	____	____
carry out plans/follow-through	____	____
coach	____	____
collect payments/money	____	____
compete	____	____
concentrate for long periods of time	____	____
conduct meetings	____	____
converse with others comfortably	____	____

	Can Do Now	Could Develop
cook well	⎯	⎯
coordinate events	⎯	⎯
create works of art	⎯	⎯
debate issues	⎯	⎯
delegate duties or responsibilities	⎯	⎯
design programs or procedures	⎯	⎯
edit written works	⎯	⎯
entertain	⎯	⎯
estimate costs	⎯	⎯
evaluate quality or performance	⎯	⎯
explain things	⎯	⎯
follow instructions or orders	⎯	⎯
handle details	⎯	⎯
hire people	⎯	⎯
host others/make people feel welcome	⎯	⎯
influence people	⎯	⎯
integrate ideas and information	⎯	⎯
interview others	⎯	⎯
investigate	⎯	⎯
keep records or logs	⎯	⎯
learn languages	⎯	⎯
listen attentively	⎯	⎯
make, build or fix things	⎯	⎯
make decisions	⎯	⎯
make friends easily	⎯	⎯
make plans	⎯	⎯
manage people	⎯	⎯
manage projects	⎯	⎯
mediate conflicts	⎯	⎯
motivate others	⎯	⎯
negotiate/bargain	⎯	⎯
nurse or treat others	⎯	⎯
observe	⎯	⎯
organize projects or spaces	⎯	⎯
perform for an audience	⎯	⎯
play sports	⎯	⎯
proofread	⎯	⎯
raise funds for a cause	⎯	⎯
read well	⎯	⎯
research	⎯	⎯
sell	⎯	⎯

	Can Do Now	Could Develop
serve as a liaison	____	____
serve others	____	____
speak to groups	____	____
summarize information	____	____
supervise others	____	____
teach or train	____	____
translate languages	____	____
troubleshoot	____	____
use computers	____	____
use mechanical abilities	____	____
visualize physical spaces or designs	____	____
work with my hands	____	____
write creatively	____	____
write essays or reports	____	____
others:	____	____

After you've checked off the skills you possess, go back and circle the ones which you think will be the real selling points for getting the job you've targeted. These should also be the skills you'd *like* to use on a job.

Now record these in the *I Can* section of the Skills Profile.

Again, have someone who knows you well review your list. You might gain some insight into undiscovered skills.

What if I don't have any skills that I'm an expert at?

Let's take conflict resolution as an example of a skill. You don't need to win a Nobel Peace Prize to be able to confidently say that you're skilled at mediating conflict. You just need to have some ability in this area and be able to back it up with concrete examples of when you've successfully mediated conflict in the past. It may be that you were known as the resident advisor who was the best mediator in your college residence hall, preventing many late night fights among your hallmates. Or maybe you took a continuing education class in alternative methods for conflict resolution during the summer. Whatever the skill, think out of the box about what you can do and how you can prove it.

The *I Know* Skills

Your *I Know* skills are the ones that are likely to be the most unique to you and your experiences. To identify your *I Know* skills, reflect on your experiences and accomplishments in the following categories, then complete the phrase "I know how to…" Try to think of academic subjects you have excelled in or roles you have undertaken (such as captain of a team or trainer of new employees at your old job) to help you identify your *I Know* skills.

School Subjects

Job

Internships

Hobbies/Interests

Activities/Affiliations/Clubs

Home/Family Life

Once you've filled in the blanks above, select the skills that best show how you can offer interviewers what they need in a candidate. Transfer these skills to the *I Know* section of the Skills Profile.

The Skills Profile

I am

I can

I know

The key is to identify which of your specific skills in any of these categories match the skills that your interviewer highlights for the prospective position. Usually, a combination of all three kinds of skills are required for a position. Besides, the "I am, I can, I know" categories are techniques to help you define and profile your skills for an interviewer. You're not going to present your skills to an interviewer in terms of these groupings anyway. You're going to present your skills as assets that you can bring to a position.

STEP 5: DEVELOP YOUR REPERTOIRE

Jayne arrives at her interview for the same position Andrew was applying for, confident that she knows what she has to offer the employer. The interviewer asks Jayne the same question posed to Andrew, "What one thing would your last boss say about you?"

Having done her homework on the position and the organization, Jayne knows that the most important skill for the position is the ability to learn quickly. So she concisely, yet colorfully, describes her ability to learn quickly: "He would say I was a quick learner because every project he gave me I figured out quickly and completed on time. For example, I had to redesign their database to track the success of various marketing strategies and print several types of reports—all in

19

two weeks. I had never used a program like that before so I took the manual home with me for a few nights to study and then took the initiative to find someone in another department who used the program. I got her to spend a few minutes showing me parts I didn't get from the manual. That way, I learned how to do it without bothering my boss. I got the file set up and the reports printed out three days before my deadline and all the managers were very pleased."

Do the examples have to come from long experiences?

The examples can be from experiences which were as long or as short as you wish. Your use of a skill over time demonstrates your consistency and commitment to developing the skill. Also, in a relatively long experience you've probably had the chance to cultivate a skill beyond the novice level.

On the other hand, there are plenty of instances when an employer just wants to know that you have a basic familiarity with a particular skill or skills. Short experiences then become valuable to show your exposure to an area and your potential to develop it further.

Jayne then describes, in the same way, experiences with two other key skills for the position—writing and organizing projects. In between stories, the interviewer asks Jayne follow-up questions. The rest of the interview progresses smoothly and, at the end, the interviewer invites Jayne back for a second interview on the spot.

Like Jayne, you've figured out that you have at least a few marketable skills. Now you're ready to *show*—not just tell—an employer that you've developed and used these skills before. Telling an interviewer that you can do this or that well without providing hard evidence is useless. Anyone can say that they have certain qualities or are capable of doing anything. But not everyone can prove it. You need to go to an interview prepared with vivid, credible examples to back your skill claims up.

Rather than trying to anticipate all the possible questions that an interviewer may ask you and all the possible answers you could give, develop a repertoire that will enable you to answer any question you may encounter. The reason you can get away with this is that most potential questions can be reduced into a handful of categories. There may be an infinite number of ways an interviewer can word a question, but there are a finite number of issues that they typically raise. For example, the following questions are really all asking the same thing: Tell me about yourself. What are three adjectives that describe you? What are your strengths and weaknesses? Why should we hire you? Why would you be right for this job?

Is it better to draw upon my school, work, or my extracurricular activities for examples?

All three are good sources for examples of skills. Recent, meaningful situations that you can speak about fully are generally the best choices. Relevant situations in any realm of your life are also key. Experience related to your field of interest is very important, so don't overlook it (even if it was part of an extracurricular or volunteer activity). Following these criteria make it easy both for you to sell yourself and for the interviewer to decide that you are the most qualified candidate.

They're all asking you to talk about your personal qualities and how these would be assets in the job. Sound familiar? It's what you did in step 4 when you put together your Skills Profile. You can now use that profile as a foundation for answering many typical interview questions. Being able to talk about yourself in terms of "I am, I can, I know" is the strategy you'll use to answer even the toughest interview questions.

The key to preparation, then, isn't to develop five different answers to the questions above. You'll only risk feeling thrown when the question ends up being asked in a sixth, unexpected way. Instead, it's better to have one general answer that's flexible enough to adapt to various specific questions.

To supplement your Skills Profile think of specific examples that back up what you say about yourself. Anyone can give a general answer. Only a strategic candidate will use hard evidence. For example, Jayne gave a winning answer to the question: "What one thing would your last boss say about you?" Andrew's response provided a lousy answer: "She would say I was a quick learner." A mediocre answer would be just the first half of Jayne's answer:"She would say I was a quick learner because any project she gave me I figured out quickly and got done on time."

To develop your personal repertoire, first pick two skills from each category of your Skills Profile and write them below:

I am: 1)

          2)

I can: 1)

          2)

I know: 1)

          2)

Now think of five examples from work, school, or extracurricular activities that demonstrate one or more of the above skills and write a few sentences about each one of them below:

1)

2)

3)

4)

5)

You want to prepare a mental archive of at least five examples like these that represent accomplishments and challenges and illustrate your best qualities. These examples of your skills constitute your repertoire.

Your repertoire should include four key elements: (1) Specific terms taken from your Skills Profile that relate to you and are relevant for the job; (2) Several examples that illustrate those qualities from your profile and that bring to life the experiences listed on your resume. The examples can be taken from work experiences (paid and unpaid), academic work (e.g., group projects, major written assignments, oral presentations, etc.), activities or sports, and occasionally from your personal life. Try to have at least one or two examples that fit each of the following categories: a) an honor or accomplishment; b) a challenge you overcame; c) an ethical dilemma you resolved; d) an innovative approach to something; e) a team-oriented activity; and f) a solo activity that showed perseverance and autonomy; (3) At least one or two facts about the organization that relate to your interests, skills, and potential, so that you can spell out for the interviewer how you would be a good fit for the job and the company; (4) Two or three bits of general knowledge about current events relevant to the job or simply relevant to being an informed adult. These may be recent happenings in local or world affairs or industry-specific developments. You don't have to be an expert on everything, but read—or at least watch—enough news to be able to carry on an intelligent conversation.

What if my repertoire illustrates many different skills?

It's likely that your most solid examples will illustrate more than one skill. That's fine. Remember, though, that the purpose of your repertoire is to ground specific skills that relate to your prospective position. When you relate your repertoire to an employer, focus on these skills. If you try to communicate all of your skills, you'll probably get off on a tangent and tell a long-winded story, diluting the strength of your strategy to help the employer understand and remember why you're skilled. So keep your agenda focused on the most relevant skills for a particular position—and use your repertoire to sell your ability to use these skills.

With these four elements in your repertoire, you'll be able to answer any question effectively and also make that all-important small talk. To make you feel a little more comfortable with the repertoire approach, there are lists of typical questions in chapter 2.

STEP 6: GET THE EDGE WITH CBO

It's two days before the interview for Paul's dream job. Even having developed a solid repertoire, he knows that he needs an easy way to help him implement it. Especially the second element—examples that illustrate his skills. From his past experience, he knows that he tends to be long-winded and unfocused when telling about his experiences. He talks to a friend who helps him realize that when he's nervous, he sometimes goes blank and fails to make clear the key elements of what situation he faced, how he acted, and what happened.

The day of the interview finally arrives. To begin their discussion, the interviewer asks him, "Why should I hire you?" Paul knows that the most important skills for the position are his research skills under pressure. So he chooses the example of his undergraduate research assistantship from his repertoire to prove these skills to the interviewer.

Then Paul reminds himself of what his friend told him. He tells the interviewer, "I worked as a research assistant to my advisor during my senior year in college. She was working on a grant-funded research project with a very tight deadline. If she missed the deadline, her grant would not be renewed and she would jeopardize her pending tenure at the university. The week of the deadline I had final exams, so the pressure was really on to meet both of my obligations.

"I took the initiative to clarify my advisor's priorities for my work that week. Then I combined my efforts with the other research assistant to use her computer programming abilities and my analysis skills to crunch some late-breaking data for the project, which would make the advisor's job easier. And I worked all weekend to get everything done.

"At the end of the week, the advisor was pleased with the quality of my work and she made the project deadline. She also praised my initiative, commitment, ability to work as part of a team, and focus under pressure."

The interviewer is very engaged in Paul's story and impressed by his demonstrated skills. Paul feels, for the first time, that he has effectively communicated his repertoire and that he really has a shot at this position.

How in depth do I need to get when I use the CBO technique with an employer?

Give enough detail to hook an employer but not so much that you go on and on. Tell your story concisely, for no more than a few minutes at a time, highlighting your skills that relate to the position's key requirements. Then stop. If the interviewer wants to know more, she'll ask you questions and you can respond accordingly. The more descriptively and clearly you tell your story, the more you'll peak the listener's curiosity.

An easy, powerful way to maximize your repertoire is to use Paul's approach, called the CBO technique. Apply this technique to your repertoire from step 5 by: (1) C: Identifying a relevant *challenge* you have encountered; (2) B: Pinpointing a corresponding *behavior or behaviors* that you used to address this challenge; and (3) O: Summarizing the preferably quantifiable *outcome* that resulted from your behavior.

Practice framing your repertoire examples from step 5 in terms of CBO by writing a few words about each element of CBO below:

Repertoire Example #1
C (Challenge):

B (Behavior):

O (Outcome):

Repertoire Example #2
C (Challenge):

B (Behavior):

O (Outcome):

Repertoire Example #3

C (Challenge):

B (Behavior):

O (Outcome):

Repertoire Example #4

C (Challenge):

B (Behavior):

O (Outcome):

Even if you're asked to describe a situation in which you failed, this technique will work. You can identify the challenge, describe your behavior, and explain the outcome. In this way you can demonstrate that you have a clear understanding of what happened and why. And then you can move the discussion forward to how you've incorporated your learning from this situation into your subsequent experiences.

STEP 7: TRY IT OUT

Sara walks into the interviewer's office and sits down in the chair across from him. Like a song you hear on the radio in the morning and can't get stop singing to yourself all day, Sara's CBO technique practice lines are echoing in her head. Distracted by the ongoing soundtrack, she jumps in before the interviewer has barely finished the first question and begins reciting her prepared lines. Sara races through her response in a monotone, eager to get the words out. Relieved that she has remembered everything word for word, she sits back and waits for the next chance to spit back her answers.

The interviewer pauses, looks at Sara quizzically, and encourages her to just relax. She continues responding mechanically and manages to make it through the interview with a response for every question. The interviewer barely registers what she's saying because he's too turned off by the fact that she's sounding very artificial, stiff, and inaccessible. Privately, he wonders about Sara's professionalism and oral communication skills. Thanking her for coming in, he ushers Sara to the door and that's the end of it.

What's the difference between practicing my CBO technique and memorizing it?

One way to think about it is to pretend you're a jazz musician. You practice your scales often. And you have jam sessions where your improvise with other musicians. When you perform and it's time to improvise, you draw upon your past experience to be confident and let it rip. Similarly, you practice your repertoire often. And you have mock interviewing sessions where you use your CBO techniques with others.

It's inevitable that you'll have difficulty expressing some things and answering some questions. Be patient with yourself as you fine tune the rough parts. And remember that real life interviewing is another way to get used to this unusual type of conversation. Don't waste employers' time interviewing for jobs you don't even want just to get interview practice. You will find, though, that interviewing for jobs that do interest you serves as a way to practice until that much sought-after offer comes along.

In fact, some entry-level job seekers with little or no interviewing experience make sure not to schedule appointments with their top choice of prospective employers until they've had a chance to practice elsewhere. This strategy works well for more experienced interviewers, too, if you're feeling rusty.

Unless you're auditioning for a role in a play, movie, or television show, your interview shouldn't be an acting exercise. And even then, a good actor or actress certainly puts more feeling into it then Sara did in the example above. You'll probably blow it if you go in with a script, which you have memorized, and repeat it to the interviewer. The script approach will make you so preoccupied with getting the words right that you'll sound fake. And this tactic won't allow you to customize your experience and education to fit the particular interview.

Again, one of the benefits of the CBO technique is that it enables you to get very comfortable relaying your repertoire. So practice your CBO technique before an interview. Just don't get hung up on saying the same things exactly the same way every time. Trust yourself to be articulate. The more practice you have using the technique in interviews, the better you'll get.

Participate in a mock interview through your college career counseling center or with friends and family. Use the list of typical interview questions in chapter 2, step 5. These questions are grouped into categories such as "Questions about your experience" and "Questions about your goals." You'll see that there are really only a few basic interview questions and many different ways to phrase these same questions. And by applying the CBO technique to your repertoire, you can answer any question without breaking a sweat.

When you're done with each response, ask for feedback on your responses and record it. Make sure you ask how what you said, as well as other elements of your presentation, came across. Your tone of voice as well as your facial expressions and other non-verbal cues will send important messages to an interviewer.

It's especially important that your non-verbal, or body language, and verbal messages match. As you can see from the descriptions of interviewers' non-verbal reactions to candidates throughout the vignettes in this chapter, you need to be aware of the messages that you send. Imagine what happens when you tell an interviewer in an enthusiastic tone that you're very excited about the position while you're subtly shaking your head no, crossing your arms across your chest, and leaning back in your chair. You would be sending mixed messages about your true level of interest. And chances are, the interviewer will only register the negative impression your body language communicates.

STEP 8: PACK YOUR BAG

The trouble starts from the moment Dan steps into the lobby of his interviewer's office building. On his way through the lobby, he looks down and notices that he has an olive oil stain from lunch at the bottom of his tie. Hoping he can get away with pretending that it's part of the pattern, he gets on a crowded elevator and presses the button for the fifth floor.

On the way up, he wonders why the others are clustering on the opposite side of the car. He doesn't realize that his breath reeks of the garlic he had eaten on his pasta at lunch and dismisses the thought as paranoia. He announces himself to the very cordial receptionist. She offers him a mint from the jar on her desk and leans forward slightly, whispering that he has a piece of hair sticking straight up at the back of his head. He thanks her and goes to the restroom to slick it down. While leaning over the restroom sink, a contact lens pops out of his eye and disappears down the drain.

Dan thinks to himself that Murphy's Law has struck again and wonders why something always goes wrong when he has an interview. With his cowlick threatening to creep back up, a hopefully invisibly spotted tie, temporarily masked garlic breath, and vision in only one eye, he makes his way back to the reception area feeling like a mess.

He follows the interviewer into an office confident that all that possibly can go wrong has already done so. A lush, flowering plant graces the edge of the desk closest to Dan's chair. Unfortunately, Dan is highly allergic to flowers. Before he has a chance to ask the interviewer politely to move the plant, Dan starts sneezing uncontrollably. The interviewer gets the clue, offers Dan a tissue, and moves the plant.

When the sneezing finally stops, the interviewer asks Dan for a hard copy of his resume to replace the fax copy. Dan doesn't have one with him but offers to send one later that day. The interviewer seems surprised, but continues with the rest of the interview. Despite all of his earlier setbacks, Dan manages to sell himself with solid responses. The interviewer is impressed by his answers and, at the end, asks for a list of references. Dan doesn't have a typed list or even notes on his references' addresses and phone numbers with him. So he tells the interviewer that he will send his reference list with the copy of his resume.

The interviewer thanks him and the interview ends. Dan leaves feeling relieved but rattled. He knows that he has jeopardized what could have been a relatively easy interview for him by arriving without either basic materials, like extra copies of his resume and a reference list, or an emergency kit with an extra tie, breath mints, comb, extra pair of contacts or glasses, and handkerchief or tissues. He also realizes that he should have opted out of a messy, smelly lunch entree and checked himself out in a mirror before showing up at the interview.

Your initial reaction to this story may be that it's pretty funny and, besides, this stuff could never happen to me. Or at least not so many things all at once. But think about how nerves, rushing, and typical interview day flukes can happen to anyone. Then you'll realize that things happen. And the kind of mishaps that Dan experienced can be avoided or fixed quickly and painlessly with only a minimum of preparation.

You probably wouldn't even go on vacation without bringing a suitcase, or at least a small bag with your clothes, toiletries, and travel arrangements. So why would you even consider showing up at an interview without the necessary back-up materials? Going to an interview packed for action is as important as practicing your CBO technique, getting dressed thoughtfully, and getting there on time.

There are some common items that you'll need every time. They include: several copies of your resume on good paper; your reference list and/or copies of reference letters; a copy of your transcript(s) if you have them; your interview cheat sheet(s); tissues or a handkerchief; a pad of paper and professional-looking pen; an organizer or datebook; and an emergency kit with safety pins, breath mints, a mirror, pantyhose or a tie, a comb or brush, and a spare pare of contacts or glasses if applicable. In addition, if you have a portfolio, remember to bring it. Anything else that makes you feel comfortable and prepared is helpful to bring with you too.

All of this stuff needs to fit into one reasonably-sized bag. A soft or hard briefcase, leather backpack, or other neat, professional bag is appropriate. Less is better. You don't want to walk into an interview overloaded with multiple bags, even professional ones. And shopping bags are definitely out. Save your errands for another time.

Many people, especially in cities, wear sneakers or casual shoes to commute and then change into good shoes when they get to work. If you do this, either wear your good shoes directly to the interview or change discreetly in a corner of the lobby or restroom and put them away in your bag before you enter the office. But don't carry your sneakers or other shoes bulging in a too small briefcase or in an extra bag. It looks tacky.

Another common problem is bad weather. Depending on what part of the country you live in, you may be more likely than not to go to an interview wishing you had a wetsuit. If, despite your best preparations, you get drenched in either the rain or snow don't automatically cancel an interview. That is, unless you get stuck because of a flooded road or white-out blizzard.

When you get to the interview site, make your first stop the restroom and dry off as best as you can. If you have the time and resources, stop into a store and buy some new clothes. Otherwise, dry off and know that your interviewer probably got caught in the same mess. Handling the situation practically and with a sense of humor is the best way to go. It also shows how you deal with unexpected situations.

How should I prepare my reference list?

Whoever your references are, it's very important that you talk with them before including them on the list. You need both to ask them permission to do so and to warn them that they might be getting calls or letters from your interviewers.

The format of the actual list should follow that of your resume in that you should ideally use the same color and weight of paper as well as the same type style. Start by putting your name, address, and phone number at the top of the page as you did on your resume and label the page "References." Then list each reference giving their first and last name, job title or academic title, name of the organization or school where they work, office address, and phone number. It's also helpful in some cases to write a brief sentence or two clarifying your connection to this person, as illustrated in the sample on the next page. This is especially important if the information on the list doesn't directly correspond to experiences on your resume.

HELEN CARR
230 Granite Street • Medesto, CA 90210
(213) 555-5555

References

Dr. Sue Smithers
Professor, Dept. of Oceanography
Water University
123 Ocean Court
Sea Island, CA 90222
(310) 777-7777
Supervisor of research assistantship, 1993-1994.

Dr. Gene Henry
Dean of Students
Water University
123 Ocean Court
Sea Island, CA 90222
(310) 777-7778
Worked with Dr. Henry as member of Student-Faculty Curriculum
Development Committee, 1993-1994.

Mr. John Smith
Owner, Smith Deli
476 Layland Drive
Catalina Island, CA 91111
Immediate supervisor in summer job, 1990-1994.

Ms. Nancy Horowitz
President
Deep Sea Explorations
111 Conch Shell Road
Marina Bay, CA 90000
(310) 444-4444
Ms. Horwoitz was formerly Senior Research Associate with the Marina Bay
Aquarium. Worked with her as Research Assistant, 1994-1995.

Step 9: Hang Loose

Wanting to be thoroughly ready, Stephanie spent every free minute through the night before her 9:00 A.M. interview doing research and practicing questions. She was busy at work and in her personal life, so she stayed up past 1:00 A.M. drilling herself. Looking exhausted and feeling wired from her intense preparation, Stephanie couldn't focus on the interview enough to have all of her pre-work pay off. She did only a mediocre job of selling herself and came across as unpolished.

Learning from her mistakes, she changed her routine before her next interview. This time she restricted her preparation to reasonable blocks of time on the days before the interview. The night before the big day she rented a comedy on videotape and went to bed early. As you'd expect, she arrived at this interview prepared, well-rested, and composed. She breezed through the interview and ultimately got the job offer.

It's easy to tell others to chill out before an interview. But actually relaxing yourself doesn't usually seem that easy. Start with your preparation. It's important to package yourself thoroughly as described in steps 1–8 of this chapter. But there's a limit. Thoroughly doesn't mean endlessly. You need to get a life too. Do what you need to do and get on with it.

The night before an interview is a time when many people get overwhelmed. Distract yourself by going to a movie, watching television, getting together with friends and having a good time. And make sure you get a good night's sleep so you look and feel refreshed during your interview.

On the big day, take some down time if you're going to an interview straight from work. Stop by a café, take a brief, peaceful walk, or find another way to get a few minutes to yourself. You want to free yourself of the chaos of the work day and clear your head so that you're on top of things during the interview.

2

During the Interview —The Self-Marketing Campaign

STEP 10: MAKE YOUR FIRST IMPRESSION WORK FOR YOU

Jared arrives in the reception area of the organization at 8:55 A.M. for a 9:00 A.M. interview. He mumbles his name to the receptionist while staring at the expensive painting hanging behind her on the wall. Expecting to go straight from the reception area into the interviewer's office, he's surprised when the receptionist hands him a clipboard with a multi-page form. Flipping through the five pages, Jared wishes that he had arrived fifteen or twenty minutes early for his interview.

He sits down again in his chair and spends the next fifteen minutes rushing to fill out an employment application. The form asks for basic information about Jared's educational and employment histories. He needs to list the names of schools, dates attended, major areas of study, and degrees received from high school forward. The application also has spaces for the names, addresses, and phone numbers of his previous employers as well as his starting and ending salaries, job titles, dates of employment, and reasons for leaving. In addition, there is a section for three personal references who aren't related to him and their phone numbers. Lines for specific information about computer and foreign language skills are other areas.

As a recent grad, Jared's work history does not easily fit into the designated categories. Part-time work, summer employment, and internships make up most of his experience. He ignores the instructions that specifically indicate that he must complete the employment section even though he's attaching his resume. Jared writes "see attached resume" and moves onto the next question.

Next, the interviewer's assistant ushers Jared into a conference room. The assistant puts a combination of brief, written aptitude tests and a personality assessment on the table in front of him. This part of the interviewing process is new to Jared, but he figures it's because he's interviewing at an exclusive consulting firm. Some of his friends who work in sales or technical fields have told him stories about these kinds of tests. But he has never expected to run into one himself.

About an hour later, the assistant returns and brings him to the interviewer's office. Frustrated by all of the paperwork, Jared greets the interviewer with a half-hearted smile and weak handshake. The interviewer initiates a few minutes of discussion about Jared's trip to the office and the weather. Jared thinks to himself, "Here we go again. More time-wasting stuff."

While there are many variations of this step in the interviewing process, Jared's experience reveals many important aspects that you should be prepared to handle. It's appropriate to arrive at your interview fifteen to twenty minutes early. This will give you time to check your appearance, relax, and fill out any necessary paperwork. Also, sometimes you may need to check in at the lobby security desk of a building. And at prime interview times there's often a long line. If you don't leave extra time, you may be late for your interview by the time you get your security pass and make your way upstairs in the elevator.

When you arrive at your interview site, make sure that you're polite to everyone. Everyone means everyone—the security guard, the elevator operator, the receptionist, assistants, and others. Besides being the courteous thing to do, you never know who the interviewer may ask for feedback about you. Or, if you're particularly rude, someone may contact the interviewer and report your behavior. Either way, you lose by being unprofessional. Client service is an integral value of almost every organization these days.And clients mean both internal and external people at all levels.The interviewer will consider your behavior during the interview visit as indicative of your future performance as an employee.

What if a "gatekeeper" (security guard, receptionist, etc.) is rude to me?

Don't respond in kind. Deal with it graciously and treat them with the same respect and courtesy that you would have if they were acting professionally. It may upset or anger you, but your contact with them is brief and you'll still come out a winner in the end.

Paperwork is an inevitable part of this stage of the interview process.Whether it's when you arrive or before you leave, you'll most likely need to fill out at least an employment application.It's a typical human resources policy because they need the form completed for their records. Be prepared to take a few extra minutes to do this without questioning or resisting the process. Follow the instructions to the letter. If the form instructs you to fill in the employment section even if you're attaching a resume, then do it. Also, print legibly. Neatness counts.

Sometimes an interviewer will ask you to take a test during the interviewing process. Possible topics include: accounting, bookkeeping, computer programming, fitness training, language translation, psychological, sales skills, management potential, organizational abilities, and drug tests. An interviewer may use such assessments to evaluate whether or not you fit the typical profile of a successful person in your prospective position, such as a sales position. Or it may be used to determine whether your personality style fits with the rest of a department.

What if you don't have all of the information you need to complete an application?

Don't panic. Just do the best you can. Write "forthcoming" in any spaces where you don't have the information handy, like a phone number. But don't leave anything blank that's not optional or intentionally put down wrong information. At the bottom of an employment application there's a statement you must sign to verify that the information you have provided is, to the best of your knowledge, accurate. If you lie on your employment application, it could be grounds for not getting hired or for getting dismissed at a later time.

One type of test that's appropriate for any level or type of position is a drug test. Many organizations have a policy of administering tests for illegal drug use to candidates who they want to offer a job. Your actual hiring may be contingent upon your having passed. The obvious strategy for this part of the interviewing process is don't do drugs and you'll pass the test. If you happen to be on prescription drugs to treat an illness or injury, make the drug test administrator aware of the situation.

The testing aspect of the process may not appeal or make sense to you. The impersonal barrage of evaluations can turn you off and make you wonder if you're in the right place. Try to give it a chance and realize that it's just the way it is at that organization. If, for some reason, you just can't bring yourself to go through such testing, then don't. But be prepared to terminate your interview at that member that it's just one part of the process.

When you finally meet the interviewer, introduce yourself with a firm handshake, consistent eye contact, and a warm smile. The first impression you make on the interviewer will set the tone for the rest of the interview. Don't underestimate the power of these easy, immediate actions. And be prepared for the interviewer to make small talk with you as a way of easing into the interview. Whenever possible stick to neutral topics like the weather, rather than controversial ones like politics.

What if I arrive at the interview site really early?

If you're more than twenty minutes early, don't go to the reception area. Take a walk around the block, find a bookstore or café, and park yourself for a little while. Just don't lose track of time or you may end up being late for the interview.

When you finally meet the interviewer, introduce yourself with a firm handshake, consistent eye contact, and a warm smile. The first impression you make on the interviewer will set the tone for the rest of the interview. Don't underestimate the power of these easy, immediate actions. And be prepared for the interviewer to make small talk with you as a way of easing into the interview. Whenever possible stick to neutral topics like the weather, rather than controversial ones like politics.

STEP 11: TARGET THE TYPE OF INTERVIEW

Christine, Sam, Pamela, Gabriel, Uma, and Frank, all college seniors, are friends who live in the same off-campus house. They go out for pizza one Friday night to trade stories from the job searching front and to give each other the inside scoop on their interviewing experiences. They've all had really different types of interviews, but they're amazed to discover that there seem to be some basic strategies for handling any kind of interview. (You'll notice the common strategies they describe relate to preparation, control during the interview, and follow-up reflected in the steps throughout chapters 1, 2, and 3.) And they're equally happy to find out that, through trial by fire, they've learned some key tactics for nailing particular kinds of interviews.

Christine goes first, describing her experience in two on-campus interviews the day before. She had signed up previously through the Career Services Office's campus recruiting program. On the day of the interviews, Christine arrived dressed in a suit with extra, clean copies of her resume and a professional looking pen and pad in hand. Since there were many students scheduled for interviews that day, she wasn't surprised that her interviews each only lasted for about thirty minutes.

Christine knew that the interviewers were only on campus for a half a day and three days, respectively, and that they were seeing candidates back to back. So, during her interviews, she concentrated on distinguishing herself from the many other students. She really tried to make an impact on the interviewers in the short time allotted by demonstrating her abilities to be focused, concise, motivated, professional, and pleasant.

As she expected, most of the interview centered on her college experiences. The interviewer asked Christine the typical questions about her major, specific classes, extracurricular activities, why she chose her college, and how she liked it. In order to make herself stand out from all of the other history majors who play sports and like their college, Christine subtly and tactfully directed the conversation toward other typical topics like her work experiences, career goals, and personal qualities. Her strategy seemed to work; the interviewer was receptive and left the interview with new information about her that wasn't on her resume.

Next, Sam described his recent on-site interview at an organization where he really wants to work after graduation. He had arranged this interview on his own through a family contact, so it was his first one with the organization. Christine was particularly interested in Sam's story, since she knows that she might be called to her prospective company's site for a second or third interview if she passed the initial screening on campus.

Sam relayed to the group how he had made a trial run to the interview site so he'd be sure of how to get there on the actual day of the interview. He explained that, since his interview was at 9:00 A.M. on a Monday, he would have surely gotten stuck in rush hour traffic if he hadn't known to allow extra time and plan a back-up route to the site.

Having gotten into the organization through a personal contact, Sam was able to skip the human resources screening and go straight to an interview with a junior staff member in the department with the opening. This interview, though, turned out to be a screening, too. The interviewer seemed more interested in learning about Sam's credentials and experience than in learning anything about Sam as a person. They want to find out if he meets the basic qualifications for the job to determine if they should pass him along to meet with a couple of managers.

Sam discovered that it is valuable to take control of this first interview by seeing it as an opportunity to check out the organization. He took advantage of being on-site by getting a feel for the environment and the people who work there. And he asked a lot of questions that gave him information about the company, the job, and career paths within the organization. That knowledge will enable him to return in a more powerful position during future interviews.

What questions should I ask to sell myself as an interested, well-informed candidate?

Your questions should be grounded in your research and go beyond the basics of what you should have learned by reading newspaper articles or the company's annual report. Use the questions in this chapter, step 17, as guidelines for typical questions you can ask. Also, keep in mind that your questions should get more sophisticated and on target as you progress through the interviewing process.

Another key way Sam took control was to manage the closing of the interview carefully and assertively. He didn't know if the screener had the authority to ask him back on the spot or to give him an idea of his chances. So he took the initiative to find out how to proceed from that point on. He asked what would happen next, who they would be passing his resume along to, and when the position needed to be filled.

Third to go, Pamela described yet another type of interview, the phone interview. Both to save her interviewer time and because they were on opposite coasts, one organization had arranged a phone interview with Pamela. What struck her right away was how she had to depend on her voice to make a good impression. Unlike an in-person interview, she couldn't use body language to emphasize her points. She had to focus on the content of what she was saying, the way in which she said it, and the sound of her voice, without feeling too self-conscious. The advantage was that she could be wearing her favorite ripped jeans, walking around in bare feet, and making strange faces while she interviewed and the interviewer would never know.

Pamela's biggest challenge was to sound energetic and enthusiastic. She knew that she comes across as dynamic and sharp in person. But on the phone her friends sometimes told her that she sounds flat or mumbled. Naturally, she couldn't change her voice overnight, but she made an effort to speak more effectively.

Toward the middle of the phone interview, she noticed that the interviewer had been silent for a couple of minutes. Always a difficult thing to deal with in a face-to-face interview, Pamela really wasn't sure what to do about it on the phone. She wasn't sure if the interviewer was listening closely or had tuned her out and was sorting through his mail. Resisting the temptation to babble just to fill the silence, she asked, "Would you like me to elaborate on that?" The interviewer responded affirmatively, and it turned out that he was just listening carefully and taking notes on what she was saying.

The only bloopers that Pamela experienced during her first phone interview were unexpected background interruptions. She forgot that her stereo was on and had to lunge to turn it off when a loud rock song blared from her speakers at the beginning of the interview. Pamela also realized that she had forgotten about call waiting. Both she and the interviewer kept getting cut off by the incessant beeping of another call.

Explaining two different group interviews at two different organizations, Gabriel compared them both to being examined under a microscope. The first interview was just with a panel of interviewers. The second interview was with a few other candidates and several interviewers. Gabriel realized that the next time he's forewarned about a group interview he'll ask which of the two types it will be—one candidate with a panel of interviewers or a few candidates with one or more interviewers.

In both situations he discovered that eye contact and body language are critical. He avoided focusing just on one person, even when that person was doing most of the talking. As he gave his replies, he directed them to the whole group by alternating eye contact. Also, he was sure to physically position himself in such a way that he was facing all of the interviewers. He wanted to give them all the feeling that he was connecting with each of them.

Again, in both interviews, Gabriel paid extremely close attention when he was introduced to the interviewers. He then referred to each of them by name during the course of the interviews. During his second interview, he forgot one of the interviewer's names and politely asked for it again in the first few minutes of the meeting.

In a group interview, how can I effectively make contact with all of the interviewers?

Body language is key. Make eye contact with everyone and address your answers to the group rather than just to the person asking the question. Beyond that, you need to accept that you're trying to establish a connection with several different kinds of people who have varied backgrounds, personality types, and perspectives. So it's much tougher than getting in sync with just one interviewer. Just be genuine and try to build a bridge to each person. Don't become a chameleon, changing radically to fit each interviewer, or you'll come across as phony and overeager to please.

There were some tactics that he used specifically for each kind of group interview. For example, in the panel interview Gabriel tried to get business cards from each person he meets so that he can follow up with them. He also asked which person he should consider the main contact for the job. This way he streamlined his follow-up efforts and avoided pestering the panelists who weren't directly involved in the final hiring decision.

In the multiple-candidate interview, he was aware that the interviewers were judging him heavily on how he got along with the other candidates and what role he took in the group. The challenge in this situation was that he didn't have as much opportunity to pitch himself, especially since much of this group interview doubled as an information session about the organization. He was hesitant to speak out too much and look like a brown-noser. Ultimately, he struck a balance between blowing his own horn and showing interest in, and cooperating with, the other applicants.

Uma described a fifth kind of interview: the unusual interview. Unusual interviews are those that don't take place at school, the office, or on the phone. She has had three unusual interviews in the last month: two at conferences and one via the computer.

Uma's first unusual interview was at a conference. She attended a national professional association conference that had special times in the schedule when she could interview with employers attending the meeting. This was a formal arrangement. She had submitted her resume before the conference to be circulated among employers and scheduled her interviews in advance. Uma tells the group, though, that she knows that at other conferences these interview sessions are sometimes less formal. Some are set up like career fairs where you wander from table to table chatting briefly with the representative and dropping off your resume.

During her second unusual interview, Uma attended a regional conference that didn't have an interview program. So she created her own on-the-spot interviewing opportunities. She met someone in the course of the conference who worked for a place that was of interest to her and arranged a meeting for a brief, exploratory interview at a café. They discussed her background and interest in the organization as well as possible areas that would be a good fit within the organization.

In both of these conference interviews, Uma discovered that the environment is generally more relaxed and casual than in traditional interview settings. The semi-vacation atmosphere of the conferences puts most interviewers in a good mood and makes the situation more conducive to conversation rather than grilling.

Uma's third interview was of an atypical type that is growing in popularity. She had a video-conference interview via personal computers. She learned that a Wisconsin-based company called ViewNet had established this system that lets interviewers (typically in large corporations) communicate with students (typically in large universities) over computers. Uma, a computer science major, reported that the process, with both sound and image transmission, is almost like being in person.

Finally, Frank takes his turn, describing his second, third, and fourth interview experiences with one prospective employer.

In follow-up interviews, which people are influential in the hiring decision?

You'll probably meet with many different levels of people, including your prospective manager's supervisor, peers, and subordinates. As organizations across industries increasingly emphasize teamwork, both within and across departments, your fit with those beyond your immediate circle of contact becomes increasingly important.

Frank's follow-up interviews were more about getting to know him, not his qualifications. Their goal was to assess his fit with the job, the organization, and his prospective colleagues. During these interviews, he met with many people involved in the hiring decision to see if they thought they could get along with him.

Follow-up interviews are time-consuming and tedious. They involve many hours and many people. Despite the challenging nature of these interviews, Frank tried to treat each encounter with enthusiasm and assertiveness. He didn't assume that each person knew what he'd told the others. He gave his sales pitch to each one and tried to stay fresh. And he kept track of the names of everyone he met for later reference.

During the course of his follow-up interviews, the length and format varied greatly but often included some activity other than straight interviewing. He went to lunch with both individuals and groups so that they could get to know him better. These lunches were sometimes nerve-racking, because he had to remain professional while eating. Not an easy task.

One tactic that Frank believes was particularly effective during his follow-up interviews was to ask thoughtful, informed questions. Interviewers want to know that candidates are thoughtful, attentive, and interested when it gets to the final stages. Also, Frank needed to get all the information he could to evaluate the potential job offer.

Step 12: Go With the Flow

Phoebe arrives at her interview prepared to answer any question and excited to ask several herself. The interviewer has a conversational tone and begins by describing the position in detail. She encourages Phoebe to react to the position description. Phoebe feels at ease because of the interviewer's casual style. She tells the interviewer what she can bring to the position and asks a few questions for clarification. Based on one of Phoebe's questions about how the position fit into the department, the interviewer makes a natural transition into discussing the department and organizational structure. During the course of this discussion, Phoebe and the interviewer exchange more questions and reactions.

At one point, Phoebe and the interviewer discover that they were members of the same sorority in college. Phoebe, feeling even more comfortable, lets her professional guard down and shares some stories about their sorority that aren't relevant to the interview. Both she and the interviewer bond on more of a personal level during this time.

Phoebe glances at her watch and notices that forty-five minutes have gone by already during this untraditional interview. Phoebe is used to an interviewer going down a list of questions and asking her if she has any questions at the end. She wonders how the interview is going, considering that she's never had an interview like this before. And they've only covered half the ground that Phoebe is used to covering in other interviews.

The interviewer ends the interview five minutes later with a warm handshake and a hearty, "Thank you for coming." Still not sure what's up, Phoebe reciprocates the handshake and thank you and reiterates her interest in the position.

Since you can never be sure what style an interviewer will have, you need to become familiar with the various possibilities before an interview. Phoebe found herself in a conversational interview, which is characterized by a casual tone and free-associating agenda. Phoebe's big mistake was to get too comfortable, telling personal stories rather than steering the interview toward issues and points she wanted to cover. She could have easily done this while maintaining the conversational style of the interview.

Isn't bonding good on common background like sororities, fraternities, and hobbies? FAQ

Sure, it's helpful to find common ground. But don't fall into gossiping about people, events, or other more personal matters. Even if the discussion seems to be going well, it reflects poorly on you and moves the interview out of the professional realm into the personal arena. It's true that an interviewer needs to find you likable, but they don't need to be your best friend. So be careful. There's often a fine line between professional and personal. And if the interviewer steers the conversation into the more personal zone on one of these common ground topics, then take the responsibility for steering it back on course.

Also, a safer example of common ground is membership in a professional organization. Then you can discuss a recent lecture you both attended on a hot issue in the field. And follow-up with how this issue may impact on the organization.

Whatever style an interviewer adopts, it probably falls into one of five categories: the Structured Interview, the Unstructured Interview, the Conversational Interview, the Confrontational Interview, or the Sales Pitch Interview.

The Structured Interview

This is the classic human-resources textbook type of interview, in which you're asked typical questions, possibly even from a form that the interviewer is filling out as you talk. The interview follows a fairly coherent line of questioning covering all of the main topics like education, work, strengths and weaknesses, and career goals. Often people who conduct this type of interview have little experience interviewing. Or it occurs in situations where interview procedures need to be standardized to elicit the same information from all candidates. This kind of interview is usually pretty easy to handle since it's likely to mirror your practice sessions and rarely conceals any hidden agendas. Be careful, though, not to come across as a robot churning out answers without conviction.

The Unstructured Interview

Some interviewers take a much looser approach to the process. They may ask many of the traditional questions but the questions seem to come in a random order not building on each other. This is often the case with inexperienced interviewers or busy people who have other things on their mind and haven't thought through what they want to ask you. The danger here is that the interviewer will end up not really knowing anything about your credentials or potential. If the conversation is all over the place, you may need to tie up loose ends for them. Spell out what you have to offer and why you'd be a good fit for the job.

How can I take control of an unstructured interview?

You don't want to end up in a power struggle with the interviewer. Especially because an inexperienced interviewer may feel threatened, rather than impressed, by such a stance. And a preoccupied interviewer may be unwilling or unable to follow your lead. As you go along or at the end, connect your main selling points and summarize how they make you the top candidate for the job. This approach will make you come across to the interviewer as articulate, focused, and able to meet their needs without upsetting the balance of power between you and the interviewer.

The Conversational Interview

Some interviewers go from the opening chit-chat to a discussion of international politics or where to go for the best hiking trails or to get the best quesadilla in town. Somehow, they skip the whole part about why you majored in philosophy. Or what you did on your last job. Or why you should get the job. You might leave the interview on cloud nine, feeling like the two of you became fast friends, but remember they're hiring a worker not a friend. Say, for example, a question about your art history major leads to a discussion of the image of the rhinoceros in seventeenth century Moroccan painting. Get in a few plugs for that award-winning thesis you wrote or that challenging internship you had at a museum.

What if I can't get a word in edgewise during the sales pitch interview?

Politely tell the interviewer that you'd like to mention one thing before you leave. And then concisely pitch to him how your skills relate to what he's been talking about the whole time. And if you have any questions, ask them. Then thank the interviewer for his time.

If, for some reason, the interviewer doesn't let you talk at all or complete what you want to say, thank him for his time. Raise your points in a thank you letter and take the opportunity to really sell how you can meet their needs. You may even want to mention that you're a good listener who can quickly understand and synthesize key information. Just *don't* be snide, (no matter how frustrated you are) and make sure that active listening is a main asset to the job. Sometimes interviewers just like to hear themselves talk, and sometimes they're testing you. So go with the flow.

The Confrontational Interview

Also called a stress interview, these situations are likely to arise when you're interviewing for jobs in high-pressured, fast-paced environments. Testing out how you react to stress in the interview gives the prospective employer an idea of how you'd handle the real thing. If you find that the interviewer is being confrontational, putting you on the spot, disagreeing with everything you say, and asking you to solve hypothetical problems in seconds, don't take the aggression personally. Also, don't worry about exactly how you answer a particular question or whether your opinion on an issue is objectively right. The content of what you say is not as important as how you handle yourself under pressure. Show that you can think on your feet, but also remain calm and composed. Then breathe a sigh of relief when it's over.

The Sales Pitch Interview

In some cases, an interview is not really an interview at all. It's more of a chance for the recruiter to sell you on the company. Rather than answering questions about yourself, you may find yourself listening to a lengthy description of the job and an enthusiastic endorsement of why XYZ Company is such as great place to work. Then, when the time is almost up, they'll say, "So, do you have any questions?" How could you after they've told you more than you'd ever want to know? If you find yourself in this situation, look for opportunities to direct the discussion toward you before it's over. Take the information you've learned and relate it to what you have to offer as well as what you're looking for.

What if the interviewer asks me directly to share a negative experience?

This is a fairly common, tough question. For example, they may ask you to tell them something about a difficult boss. Or they make ask you to describe a failure. If you must discuss a negative experience, be as neutral as possible—never bitter. And talk about how you resolved it and what you learned from the experience. The interviewer really wants to know how you handle difficult situations as well as what you've learned from them. These insights will help the interviewer determine how you're likely to handle challenges in the future.

Step 13: Manage the Interview

There are several guiding principles that will enable you to manage any interview, no matter what type or style you encounter. It's easy to confuse managing with either dominating or yielding to the interviewer. Neither extreme works best. The most effective strategy is to build a respectful, professional relationship with the interviewer. Within this framework, you can make your move and sell yourself as the winning candidate.

Below, you'll find some solid tips for keeping your interview on track:

- When you're in an interview, don't assume anything. Listen *carefully* to the interviewer. If a question requires a complex response, it's fine to take a few seconds to reflect instead of just blurting out a response. As you saw in the phone interviews section (chapter 2, step 11), silence isn't your enemy. Don't rush to fill it.

- Don't monopolize the conversation or avoid answering questions. There are many ways to take control subtly without ticking the interviewer off and starting a power struggle. Be creative.

- Be positive about everything and everyone. Not fake, rah-rah positive, but not dumping on your boss for treating you unfairly, how boring your job is, and how stupidly your co-workers behave. Even an offhanded negative comment in the midst of a bunch of positive ones will stand out and concern the interviewer. They may be tempted to dig deeper into your comment and find a reason to take you out of the running. Or your attitude alone may do it. Besides, it's always a bad idea to burn bridges. You shape your professional reputation every time you come into contact with someone in your field. Even if it's for an interview that doesn't lead to a job.

- Don't copy the interviewer's body language position for position. It might be noticed and seem you're making fun of them or acting strangely. You can, though, try to match the general posture of the interviewer and thereby become more physically comfortable.

- Don't let a case of the interview jitters sabotage your meeting. When you feel nervous, try to remember that the interviewer may be just as nervous or inexperienced as you. Also, remember that an interview is just a conversation.

What do I do if I encounter a cultural difference with my interviewer?

Well, let's take the example of Sabrina. Sabrina greets her interviewer, a married orthodox Jewish man: In an effort to respect what she thinks is his cultural belief not to touch women besides his wife, she doesn't extend her hand. The interviewer, though, extends his hand. After a long pause, she awkwardly shakes it. Embarrassed, she mumbles an apology about not wanting to offend him.

Although Sabrina had the best of intentions, she misjudged the situation based on the interviewer's looks. The safest thing to do in any situation where there might be cultural differences is to follow the lead of the interviewer. Be prepared for the unexpected and act accordingly. Just because someone looks different doesn't necessarily mean that they have a different standard of behavior. Also, there are many variations on cultural behavior. So it's impossible to anticipate all of them.

- Don't let the interviewer do all of the work. Back up all of your responses with evidence. Never give a yes/no or one-word answer to a question. You can begin your response with one word, then elaborate appropriately.

- Unless the interviewer brings them up first, avoid taboo subjects like salary, benefits and the like because it makes you look like you're only interested in picking up your paycheck, and not the job itself. Also, it's in your best negotiating interests to wait until the last minute to discuss such items. Then you can know enough about the position to accurately rate its worth and how much value you bring to the position.

What if I space out during an interview and don't hear a question?

Most of us get tired or zone out from time to time. You may have been up late working on a project the night before an interview and just didn't get enough sleep. Don't try to explain this or any other excuse you have for drifting away. And don't blurt out, "What did you say?" If, for some reason, you zone out during an interview or don't understand what an interviewer is saying, it's okay to ask politely for a repeat or clarification. It's definitely not okay to be rude. Or disrespectful. Whether you do it on purpose or not.

STEP 14: EXPECT VARIATIONS ON THEME QUESTIONS

Aisha really wants to prepare herself for the kinds of questions that she can expect during an interview. She talks with friends, gets a handout from the career services office at her college, and leafs through some books in the library which list question after question and sample answers. Overwhelmed by the sheer volume of questions she's faced with, she wonders which ones she should really focus on. It reminds her of trying to learn huge vocabulary lists before the SAT.

As discussed in chapter 1, step 4, there are really only a limited number of core questions that an interviewer can ask you and an unlimited number of ways for them to phrase these questions. Here's a list of some typical core questions, grouped by category, that you can expect:

College experience questions

Why did you choose your major?

Which classes in college have you liked best/least? Why?

Why did you select your college? How have you liked it?

Has your college experience prepared you for a career?

Describe your most rewarding college experience.

If you could do it over, how would you plan your education differently?

What teaching styles do you react best to?

Do you plan to go to graduate school?

Are your grades a good indicator of your potential?

What have you learned from your extracurricular activities?

Tell me about one of your papers or your thesis.

Questions about you

Tell me about yourself.

How did you choose this career direction?

What are your strengths and weaknesses?

How would you describe yourself?

How would a friend or your last boss describe you?

What motivates you to work hard?

What does success mean to you?

Of what are you most proud?

In which kind of environment do you work best?

How do you handle pressure?

What's important to you in a job?

Do you have a geographical preference? Would you relocate? Travel?

Describe a major obstacle you've encountered.

What have you learned from mistakes you've made?

What would you do if you won the lottery?

What else should I know about you?

Questions about your experience

Tell me about your jobs/internships.

How did your liberal arts background prepare you for this job?

What work-related skills do you have?

What was the toughest job challenge you faced and how did you deal with it?

Questions about your goals

What do you see yourself doing five years from now? Ten? Fifteen?

What do you really want out of life?

Why do you want to work for us?

Why do you want to work in this industry?

Questions to see if you know what you're getting into

What do you know about this organization?

What do you think it takes to be successful in this organization?

Why do you want to work for us?

What do you look for in a job?

How can you make a contribution to our organization?

Where do you think this industry is headed?

Stress questions/brainteasers

Please open the window over there (and it's painted shut).

How many manholes do you think there are in this city? Why are manhole covers round?

STEP 15: SHOW OFF YOUR COMPETENCIES

You may wonder what employers are really looking for in your responses and whether you can even give it to them. The secret is competencies. These are many of the "I can" skills mentioned in chapter 1, step 4 that every kind of employer seeks in a prospective employee. And they're skills that most people have at least a few of and can prove. Some key competencies that apply to many fields are: analytical skills, computer skills, flexibility, foreign language fluency, interpersonal skills, leadership skills, oral and written communication skills, and teamwork skills.

Are some competencies more important than others?

They're all important. But, of course, you need to consider the needs of your prospective employer. While one position may have foreign language fluency as its number one requirement, another position may have teamwork as its top priority. So before you invest in an intensive language course or begin volunteering on a committee to get teamwork experience, check out specific positions. Determine which competencies seem to be consistently important to most of them. Don't spread yourself thin trying to get up to speed on too many different competencies. Pick the top ones and find easily accessible ways to work on these skills.

These "I can" skills, or competencies, are especially valuable assets for liberal arts majors, who may not feel that they have as many "I know" skills as those grads with technical, specialized majors. To launch an effective self-marketing campaign during the interview, you need to present a wide range of these abilities. So make sure that you include them in your repertoire and highlight them during your interview.

Step 16: Blurt Out, Shut Out, or Hedge Out Answers to Illegal Questions

Laurie thinks her interview is going well. She answers all of the interviewer's questions with relative ease. Then, out of the blue, the interviewer asks her, "Do you plan to have a family?" Caught off guard, Laurie isn't sure how to respond. The question doesn't seem to fit with the others, except the one about her future goals.

The organization she's interviewing with is a very family-oriented one. In fact, they design and produce children's educational software. But she's afraid that if she answers yes, then she'll either not get the job or be limited in her future growth opportunities there. And she's afraid to answer no, because then the interviewer may think that her values don't fit with the organization's. Generally, she's not comfortable with the question and feels like it's a no-win situation.

After what feels to her like a long pause, she responds, "Maybe, someday." The interviewer scribbles a note about her answer down on the pad in front of them. But Laurie isn't sure how her answer went over.

What if I'm not sure whether a question is illegal or not?

Use your best judgment. That's why the hedge it out strategy is so effective. Even if you're not sure if a question is really illegal, you can use this strategy to respond without compromising yourself. You and the interviewer both win and you can get on with the interview.

When you find yourself facing a tough question that seems irrelevant or makes you feel uncomfortable, trust your gut. Don't just dismiss your feelings and assume that it's your problem. Chances are, it's the interviewer's problem. Many interviewers won't intentionally ask you illegal questions. They may not be knowledgeable about Equal Employment Opportunity laws or they may become genuinely curious about your life and forget to be professional. Some interviewers, though, will deliberately ask you illegal questions just to see what they can get away with. In either scenario, it's not acceptable ethically or legally.

It's your responsibility to determine if a question is illegal. Sometimes this can be tricky, because most of us aren't employment lawyers who can spot a problem question right away. That's why it's important to familiarize yourself with some common illegal and legal questions asked about various aspects of your background. Here are some sample ones to help you get started:

Inquiry Area	Illegal Questions	Legal Questions
National Origin/Citizenship	Are you a U.S. citizen? Where were you/your parents born What is your "native tongue"?	Are you authorized to work in the United States? What languages do you read, speak, or write fluently? *(This question is okay, as long as this ability is relevant to the performance of the job.)*
Age	How old are you? When did you graduate from State University? What's your birth date?	Are you over the age of 18?
Marital/Family Status	What's your marital status? Who do you live with? Do you plan to have a family? When? How many kids do you have? What are your child care arrangements?	Would you be willing to relocate if necessary? Travel is an important part of the job. Would you be able and willing to travel as needed by the job? *(This question is okay, as long as ALL applicants for the job are asked it.)* This job requires overtime occasionally. Would you be able and willing to work overtime as necessary? *(Again, this question is okay as long as ALL applicants for the job are asked it.)*
Affiliations	What clubs or social organizations do you belong to?	List any professional or trade groups or other organizations that you belong to that you consider relevant to your ability to perform this job.
Personal	How tall are you? How much do you weigh?	Are you able to lift a 50-pound weight and carry it 100 yards, as that is part of the job? *(Questions about height and weight are not acceptable unless minimum standards are essential to the safe performance of the job.)*

Inquiry Area	Illegal Questions	Legal Questions
Disabilities	Do you have any disabilities? Please complete the following medical history. Have you had any recent or past illnesses or operations? If yes, list and give dates. What was the date of your last physical exam? How's your family's health? When did you lose your eyesight? How?	Are you able to perform the essential functions of this job with or without reasonable accommodation? *(This question is okay if the interviewer has thoroughly described the job.)* As part of the hiring process, after a job offer has been made, you will be required to undergo a medical exam. *(Exam results must be kept strictly confidential, except medical/safety personnel may be informed if emergency medical treatment is required, and supervisors may be informed about necessary job accommodations, based on the exam results.)* Can you demonstrate how you would perform the following job-related functions?
Arrest Record	Have you ever been arrested?	Have you ever been convicted of _____? *(The crime named should be reasonably related to the performance of the job in question.)*
Military	If you've been in the military, were you honorably discharged?	In what branch of the Armed Forces did you serve? What type of training or education did you receive in the military?

From National Association of Colleges and Employers in "Illegal Questions: What's the Right Answer?" *(Planning Job Choices, 1996)*

When you've determined that a question is illegal, you have three strategic choices of how to respond: *blurt it out, shut it out, or hedge it out.* If you choose to blurt it out, or respond directly, then you get it over with. But you also risk telling the interviewer something about yourself that takes you out of the running. If you choose to shut it out, or refuse to answer, then you protect your rights. But you also risk offending the interviewer and, again, weakening your candidacy.

The third strategy, hedge it out, is the least risky option. You can respond to the concern behind the question without giving away any inappropriate or uncomfortable information. For example, Laurie could have chosen to hedge it out by saying, "Whatever type of lifestyle I choose in the future, I plan to be committed to a career and to this first job." In this way, she would address the interviewer's potential concern about whether or not her career is her top priority. At the same time, Laurie wouldn't have to disclose her potential plans specifically or dignify an illegal question.

What if the interviewer intentionally asks me one illegal question after another?

FAQ

If you can't seem to redirect the interview and are becoming increasingly uncomfortable, then you may consider confronting the interviewer. If they still persist, then it's okay to end the interview and leave. This is hopefully a rare situation, but you never know. You probably wouldn't even consider working for an individual or an organization that treats you this way during an interview anyway.

STEP 17: SELL YOURSELF, GATHER KEY INFORMATION, AND EVALUATE A JOB BY ASKING GREAT QUESTIONS

Doug thinks he's sailing through his interview with no problems. The interviewer, an inexperienced recruiter, uses a structured style and goes down a list of traditional questions, one by one. He answers all of the interviewer's questions, dismissing each one from his mind as he moves on to the next one. The interviewer doesn't pause between each of Doug's answers and the next question. So Doug and the interviewer alternate talking, like a volley during a tennis match. At the end of the interview, the interviewer asks Doug if he has any questions. Doug decides that he's said and heard enough, so he responds, "No." The interviewer thanks him for his time and ends the interview. Doug leaves satisfied that he's a done a great job of selling himself.

What Doug didn't know is that even the most inexperienced interviewer expects a candidate to ask questions throughout the interview as well as at the end of the interview. Asking good questions throughout an interview helps you sell yourself in many different ways. For example, you demonstrate your interest in the organization and position as well as your professional curiosity. These are important qualities to employers. Secondly, you gather key information about the job and organization that will enable you to refine your sales pitch as you go. The more you understand about the interviewer's priorities, the more you can tailor what you have to offer to the employer's needs. Finally, the input you get from the interviewer will help you to better evaluate the job and whether or not you want to pursue a potential job offer.

Doug's approach wasn't strategic, and he made a weak impact by just answering questions mechanically. It's like he was present physically, but wasn't fully present mentally. Doug should have shown the interviewer that he was interested by initiating some questions and engaging him in conversation. A good interview is not a one-sided effort. It's a two-way discussion.

What kinds of questions shouldn't I ask?

Questions that are irrelevant to the job or organization. Stay away from marginal queries about competitors, other positions that don't relate to the position you're interviewing for, or current trends that have no bearing on the organization. Also, don't interrogate the interviewer about their career histories. It's okay, for example, to ask specific questions about what they like best and least about working at the organization. But don't start interviewing them beyond that. It may make them uncomfortable and you may inadvertently offend them. If the interviewer chooses to share some in-depth information about their career path or experiences at the organization, then feel free to ask follow-up questions. Just keep them open-ended and don't push it.

Here are some questions you can ask to get your creative juices flowing:

About the organization

How does your organization differ from its competitors?

What are the company's plans for future growth?

What problems is your organization facing?

What do you like most about working here?

How would you describe the corporate culture (or work environment) here?

About the job itself

Where does this position fit into the structure of the department and the organization as a whole?

What are the future plans for this department?

How much contact is there between departments or areas (if a large organization)?

To whom would I report?

What percentage of my time would be spent in the various functions you described that this job involves?

Is it organizational policy to promote from within?

What is a typical career path for people in this position?

Why is this position available?

What personal qualities make someone successful in this job?

May I talk to someone who currently holds or recently held this position? (Only appropriate if an offer has been extended or seems imminent.)

Won't the interviewer find me pushy if I take control?

No. If you act assertive, you'll score bonus points for professionalism with the interviewer. You'll demonstrate that you're genuinely interested in the position, confident in your worth, and pro-active about getting things done. And it's often easier to come across as appropriate when you're face-to-face with the interviewer then when you're on the phone following up after the interview.

STEP 18: END THE INTERVIEW ON YOUR TERMS

Hanna is relieved that her interview is over. Standing up and extending her hand for the final handshake, the interviewer says, "Well, if you have no further questions, then we're done." Hanna says, "Thank you for taking the time to speak with me. I'm very interested in the position." She shakes the interviewer's hand and walks to the door. The interviewer responds, "Fine. We'll call you." Hanna replies, "Good-bye."

Unknowingly, Hanna blew her chance to sell herself one more time and end the interview on her terms. She did thank the interviewer for her time and reinforced her interest in the position. These are important, but relatively passive acts. She should have taken control of the situation and left the door open to follow-up with the interviewer.

What if I'm not sure that this position is my first choice?

Be positive but honest. Tell the interviewer that you're very interested in the position, that you're confident that you can be an immediate asset to their organization, and that you'd like to call them next week to check on how their decision is going. Just leave out the parts about how you're available on a few days notice and how this is your first choice over all the others you're being considered for. You can pitch yourself strongly for any position that you're interested in by tailoring the end of the interview to your terms.

A strategic ending might have gone like this: When the interviewer indicated that the interview was over, Hanna could have said, "Actually, I'd like to know how I should proceed from here. Should I contact you in a few days?" Then the interviewer most likely would have said something like, "Well, we have a few more people to interview this week. Then we'll be making a decision soon." Hanna might have replied, "When would I start if I were hired?" The interviewer may have responded, "We'll need the position filled by the first of the month." Hanna then could make her big move with, "I'm available to start any time just with a few days notice. I'm very interested in this position, above any others I'm currently a candidate for, and I know I could make a contribution to this organization. Would it be all right if I call you next week to see how your decision is going?" The interviewer might respond, "That would be fine. I can't guarantee I'll have much to report, but you can try." Hanna then could say, "Great. Thanks for your time. I'll be in touch." And then she could shake hands with the interviewer and leave.

After the Interview —Follow-up to Get the Job

STEP 19: DEBRIEF THE INTERVIEW

Derrick goes home after his interview is over, changes into sweats and a T-shirt, and heads for his favorite chair. His roommate walks through the door a few minutes later and asks Derrick how his interview went. Derrick tells him that it went really well and asks him if he wants to grab a video and order some Chinese food. Satisfied that he's done all he can to get the job, Derrick smiles and thinks to himself, "Now all I have to do is relax and wait for the phone to ring."

Like Derrick, now that you've survived the interview itself you may think that your work is done. Unfortunately, you can't just kick back and decide that it's out of your hands. If you stop actively pursuing a job at this point in the process, you're making a risky choice. You may end up wasting all the time and energy you've already put into your search. And you probably don't stand a chance against your competition.

A good interview will enable you to get your foot in an organization's door. But you're only partially there. Since the interview process is often lengthy, you need to follow-up at every stage, not just after the first interview. Good follow-up will get you the job, because it lets you make sure that an employer knows that you've got what they need. It also demonstrates your genuine interest, assertiveness, and potential capacity to see work through to the end. Even if you're not necessarily the most qualified candidate for the job, good follow-up will give you an edge over other candidates.

What if everything went okay, but the interviewer didn't indicate where I stand?

If you believe that you didn't make any major bloopers with anything you said, the interviewer may have thought of you as a favorable candidate. But you may be the first or one of the first candidates they interviewed. So they may be unsure of how you'll compare with others and want to reserve judgment until they talk with more candidates.

The best tactic you can use is to brainstorm anything that you didn't say about how what you have to offer fits with what they need. Then make sure to highlight this information in your thank you letter (see step 20). This way you'll spark the interviewer's interest further as well as remind them of your other strengths.

One way to keep on top of where you are is to debrief yourself after each interview. Here are some sample questions that you can use to start:

- What did I learn from this interview about the job? the organization? the supervisor? the culture? my prospective peers?

- What was my impression of the job opportunity as a whole?

- What key organizational needs did the interviewer communicate that coincide with the position?

- How do my qualifications match these needs?

- Which aspects of my background did I emphasize and which did I neglect?

- Did the interviewer have any explicit or implicit concerns about my candidacy?

- How did I address or fail to address these concerns? Which questions did I have a hard time answering?

- Who has input into making the hiring decision? Who has the final say?

- Where do I think I stand as a candidate?

- What is the hiring time frame for the job and the next steps I need to take?

What if I met with multiple interviewers on the same day?

It's appropriate to acknowledge everyone you met with in one of two ways. One way is to write everyone a thank you note. Be sure that each letter is slightly different, because interviewers from the same organization sometimes share notes with each other or even keep them together in a file. Another way is to write one letter to the person responsible for organizing your day or the most senior level person, and ask them to thank the others. Mention the others by full name. This approach is okay if you only spoke briefly with the others.

STEP 20: POSITION YOURSELF AS THE TOP CANDIDATE

On Monday, Wendy went back to work after her interview. That evening, she debriefed herself and starting writing a thank you letter to the interviewer on her computer before falling into bed. She got busy with work and social obligations during the next few days. Late Thursday night, she pulled out some leftover white printer paper and quickly printed out her letter. She only had off-white envelopes left, so she used one of those. The next morning on her way to work, she put the letter in her corner mailbox and didn't give it another thought.

The thank you letter Wendy sent read like this (superscripts mark the places where she made mistakes):

40 East 32nd Street, Apt. 2A
New York, NY 12345

October 14, 1996

Mr. Albert H. Hockenpepper
Vice President
Wonka Tonka Entreprises[1]
1147 Madison Avenue, Suite 681
New York, NY 54321

Dear Mr. Hockenpepper:

Thank you for taking the time out of your busy schedule to meet with me yesterday concerning the Customer Service Representative position. I enjoyed having the opportunity to speak with Bob and Jane.[2] Specifically, I was impressed by your highly collaborative work environment and your initiative to further integrate the product managers and customer service representatives.

Our conversation reinforced that my experience and interests are a decent[3] fit with the position. As we discussed, my academic background in psychology,[4] two years as a front desk worker at my college's student union, and two years as a resident advisor at my college have required strong administrative, time management, and client relations skills. My experience, therefore, would enable me to add immediate value to your organization.[5]

When we discussed my resident advisor work, I am not sure I made it clear that I am the initial contact for the students[6] on my floor regarding all issues.[7] Moreover, I work as part of a team of residential advisers in my residence hall to plan activities as well as to provide crisis intervention. I would use this experience in a high volume, team environment to effectively assist you in meeting the needs of your customers.

Thank you again for the opportunity to review my candidacy for the Customer Service Rep[8] position. I am psyched[9] about the position. As you suggested, I will call you next Wednesday morning to discuss the possibility of meeting with your customer service colleagues.

Sincerely,

Wendy Tragger

Wendy's tactics undermined her ability to position herself as the top candidate for the job. She should have sent her thank you letter within twenty-four to forty-eight hours of her interview. Her delay may have cost her the job. This is especially important in this high tech age, when other candidates may send their letters by fax, E-mail, or overnight mail as well as by regular mail. Don't necessarily send a thank you letter by fax or E-mail, since it won't look polished or personal. As always, use your common sense. If you're applying for a job at a high tech company, for example, then the hiring manager may not get to her regular mail for days, but will be sure to check her E-mail. You then may want to consider using E-mail.

Also, Wendy should have printed her letter and envelope on high quality, matching bond paper. The format, as well as the content, sends a message to the employer about your level of professionalism and interest in the position. Always keep these supplies on hand in case you need them. In special cases, it's acceptable to hand-write a note on a folded card or use plain paper if the place you interviewed at was informal. Make sure your handwriting is legible if you choose this route.

If Wendy had spent more time and attention working on the content of her letter, it wouldn't have been littered with problems. As you can see, it's critical that you write a targeted, persuasive letter that convinces your prospective employer that you're the candidate they should keep pursuing and eventually hire. Wendy's letter would be a solid one except that it has nine problems. Some of them are obvious, while others are subtle.

Wendy's first mistake was a spelling one. She reversed the "r" and "e" in "Enterprises." Spelling errors are absolutely unacceptable. It's even worse, though, when you spell the interviewer's name or organization's name wrong. Address the letter to your interviewer using their correct title and address from their business card. If you've misplaced the card or didn't get it, call the receptionist at the organization and confirm the person's name, title, and mailing address.

The second mistake was less obvious. It was a plus that Wendy acknowledged the others with whom she met to the interviewer. She had the right idea when she mentioned the others by name. But she blew it by mentioning only their first names. It's possible that there's more than one Bob or Jane.

And even if there's not, it's appropriate, out of respect, to mention them each by full name.

In the second paragraph, Wendy should have proofed the first and second sentences more carefully. Her third mistake was that she used the word "decent" to describe her "fit with the position." In order to persuade the employer that you're the best candidate for the job, you need to present yourself with confidence. "Decent" doesn't imply that you believe you're right for the position. Terms like "excellent" or "good" are better choices.

In the second sentence of the paragraph, Wendy made her fourth mistake. She left an extra space between "psychology" and the comma after it. It's easy to overlook this kind mistake. But it's the type of thing that will pop out to the interviewer.

Wendy's fifth problem was in the last sentence of the second paragraph. She referred to Wonka Tonka Enterprises as "your organization." While the sentence as a whole was a powerful one, this reference diminished its power. Whenever possible, it's important to personalize your thank you letter. One way to tailor it is to use the organization's name where appropriate. Be aware, though, that it's overkill to use the name too much. So only use it in places where you don't want the employer to think you're sending a form, or generic, thank you letter.

When Wendy described her resident advisor work in the third paragraph, she mentioned the "students." This was her sixth problem, because it would be a stronger passage if she would elaborate on what she means by students. The number of students, for example, may be relevant information here. Similarly, Wendy mentioned that she dealt with the students' "issues." Her seventh mistake was that she doesn't tell the interviewer what types of issues. Given that she was applying for a customer service position, it would have been impressive for her to show that she had handled a range of relevant issues before.

In the final paragraph of Wendy's thank you letter, she abbreviated the position's title. This was her eighth mistake. Saying "Rep" instead of "Representative" is too casual for this kind of letter. You should always write out the full title of the job. Then Wendy made mistake number nine, writing that she was "psyched" about the position. Wendy changed the tone of her letter in this paragraph from formal to casual. Even when you write a thank you letter using a less formal tone, watch your word choices. Slang is never appropriate Use simple, direct language to get your points across.

In general, gear the tone and format of your letter to the style of the interviewer. If your interviewer was generally laid back, used casual language, and the workplace was relaxed, match your tone accordingly. Toward the other extreme, a very formal interview requires an equally formal thank you note. No matter what, it's safer to err on the side of being too formal, rather than too casual.

The following guidelines will enable you to write a targeted thank you letter and avoid the slip ups that Wendy made in her letter. Always begin your letter with the interviewer's proper name. Mr., Ms., or Dr. are all acceptable after the "Dear." On rare occasions, you might use the person's first name. For example, if ,during the interview, he asked you to call him by his first name, or if you knew him personally from another context before the interview.

Use Paragraph 1 to REVIEW the purpose and events of your interview. Immediately acknowledge your interviewer for meeting with you. For example, "Thank you for taking the time out of your busy schedule to meet with me yesterday...," or "It was a pleasure to meet with you today...," or "I appreciated the opportunity to meet with you today..."

Cite by full name any other members of the organization you met through your primary interviewer. "Thank you for introducing me to _____ and _____" or "It was a pleasure also meeting _____," or "I enjoyed having the opportunity to speak with _____ about (name of organization or position)."

Mention one or two specific things you learned and/or were impressed by: "I enjoyed learning more about the _____ position," or "It was a pleasure to learn more about the structure of your organization, its business philosophy, and current initiatives;" "Specifically, I was impressed by..." or "Our conversation helped me to gain a better understanding of ..."

Convince your prospective employer that you can do the job by using Paragraph 2 to HIGHLIGHT briefly any key aspects of your academic background, work experience or skill sets that are critical to the job. You can introduce these aspects in the context of your interview by saying things like, "Our conversation reinforced that my background and experience are an excellent fit with the position," or "As we discussed, my background in _____ and three years as a _____ with _____ have required strong _____, _____, and _____ skills."

Be selective. Don't repeat your entire resume or interview responses in this paragraph. You'll make a solid impression if you include those examples that support these sources of information in a new, concise way. Your thank you letter then becomes another way for you to demonstrate your abilities to exercise good judgment, to synthesize what the interviewer told you, and to communicate your understanding of how your assets match the interviewer's needs.

Whenever possible, link your attributes with the job qualifications and reinforce what you'll contribute to the organization: "My experience doing _____ will enable me to promote your _____," and "These skills would enable me to add immediate value to (name of department and /or organization)," or "Based on my experience and academic preparation, then, I would hit the ground running with (name of organization), or as a (name of position)."

Include key information that you forgot to mention during your interview by using paragraph 3 to SUPPLEMENT with any additional information about yourself. You may want to cover attributes that you didn't discuss, bring up points that you didn't fully explain, or elaborate on responses that you felt were incomplete during your interview.

If it was clear that the interviewer had reservations about your candidacy, this is your opportunity to say something to turn your situation around. You may believe that your GPA was of concern, or that the employer was troubled by your lack of direct experience. Acknowledge the hesitation and provide a strong, positive counter-argument.

Be careful, though, not to remind the interviewer that something didn't go well in the interview. Instead, state the thought in a strong, positive tone: "In addition to the skills we discussed during our meeting, I also have_____ years of experience doing _____" or "… have taken _____ courses in _____," or "I am proficient in _____ as well as in the _____ that we discussed." As in the second paragraph, make sure to get specific about and quantify your skills or accomplishments whenever possible.

End your letter from a position of strength by using paragraph 4 to MOVE FORWARD by reinforcing your interest and intentions. Make sure that you thank the interviewer again. "Thank you again for the opportunity to discuss my candidacy for the _____ position." Keep it simple here. Don't go overboard and ingratiate yourself too much or you'll sound fake and like you're kissing up.

Also, this is the place to reinforce your level of interest in the position. For example, "I am very interested in the position." Only express your enthusiasm for the position if you sincerely feel this way. If an organization is your first choice, let them know. If you don't feel enthusiastic, either say nothing or let them know diplomatically that you're not interested in going further with them in the process.

Finish the letter by referring to the next step in the process: "I look forward to hearing from you on Monday, as you mentioned, concerning the next step, or "I will call you next Wednesday, as you suggested, to discuss the possibility of meeting with your colleagues." As in the former three paragraphs, be specific. State the day and terms of the next step directly without being pushy. Make sure you refer back to your debriefing notes to determine the interviewer's cue about how to proceed.

STEP 21: MASTER THE ART OF PERSISTENCE

Sean was really excited about securing a certain job. After he sent his thank you letter he couldn't stop thinking about it. His curiosity and impatience got the better of him. So he called the employer every day for a week to check in and see how the decision process was going. He also sent the employer a thick file folder of past work samples every couple of days in Fedex packages. After the first call, Sean couldn't reach the employer on the phone. Their assistant always said they were busy and took messages. Ultimately, the employer got annoyed by Sean's inappropriate persistence and didn't offer him the job.

It's understandable that you may get eager, like Sean, to know what's up at this point in the process. But you need to keep it under control or you'll mess up all the strategic moves you've made to date. Persistence, or the degree to which you contact your prospective employer, can be a tricky part of follow-up. There's a fine line between being persistent and blowing it by being annoying. Follow what the interviewer told you about the time frame for hiring and how they planned to communicate with you. Don't, for example, call your interviewer every few days. This will be interpreted as poor judgment or desperation.

Also, if you're working through an employment agency rather than directly with your prospective employer, you'll need to direct your persistence toward the agency. As the liaison between you and the organization, the agency is responsible for keeping the communication channels open. Your recruiter will most likely contact you by phone after your interview or request that you call them to let them know how it went. They'll then call your prospective employer, get feedback about your interview, and contact you to let you know what the interviewer said about your interview as well as the next step. Use this information both to inform your thank you letter to the interviewer and how you persist strategically afterwards.

Can't I just say I'm checking in when I call, especially if I get an assistant or voicemail?

There's nothing tactical about just checking in. You need to use every contact with an interviewer as a chance to sell yourself. Let them know that you're really interested in the position and reinforce why you're the best one for the job. You can also do things like send them an article of interest related to something you discussed during your interview. Or, have a key reference call on your behalf to talk you up. Be an assertive and strategic candidate – not a passive, inquiring one.

If you decide to call the interviewer to follow-up after sending a thank you letter, be clear about why you're calling and make sure it's for a good reason. For example, you may have received another job offer and need to know where you stand. You may just be curious after a week or so about the status of your candidacy. Or, if your interview was not as effective as you'd hoped, you may want to try to make a better impression during a follow-up call and possibly keep yourself in the running. These are all acceptable reasons. It's important that you're clear in your own mind about the purpose of your call so that you can be direct with the interviewer during the call.

How soon you call after your interview depends on the reason why you're calling. In general, don't call before your follow-up letter arrives, and give your interviewers at least a few days before checking in with them. Also, carefully determine the time of the day and week you call. You're more likely to reach an interviewer either early or late in the work day. And it's better to avoid Mondays and Fridays, because the beginning and end of the work week can be hectic or vacation times.

When you do call, be courteous and brief. Focus the call on your interest in the job and your ability to do it better than anyone else. Sometimes the interviewer will indicate that he has not made a decision yet. In this case, consider your call an opportunity to keep yourself fresh in the mind of your prospective employer.

If the interviewer responds that he's decided to hire someone else, try to get feedback about why you weren't selected. Some interviewers will be more comfortable with this request than others. If he resists, thank him for his time and don't probe further. If he's receptive, take advantage of this chance to learn something from the experience and to see how you can improve your job search skills the next time.

STEP 22: GET OUT OF A RUT

Yolanda hurries home after a long day at work eager to check her phone machine for messages from interviewers. On the way up the steps she flips through her mail and is disappointed to find two rejection letters from prospective employers. This brings her total number of rejections to six in the last two weeks. She sinks into the living room sofa, feeling really down. She just can't figure out what's going wrong.

Even when you give the interviewing process all you've got, sometimes you still don't get the job offer. When that happens, it's easy to get discouraged and give up. There are many reasons why you may lose out on a job to someone else, reasons that are beyond your control. Someone else may be an internal candidate, have more targeted qualifications, or be better connected through a network. These reasons don't mean that you wouldn't be an asset to an organization or that you couldn't do a job. They just mean that it didn't work out this time.

Rejection can feel devastating and you may want to go off on an indefinite vacation, hide out in your home, or escape into a movie marathon surrounded by as much junk food as you can stand. Feeling down is understandable, but you can't let it stop you. Acknowledge it and realize that it's a normal reaction to not getting something you really want.

It's important to cope with your lows during the interviewing process as they happen, so that you can move on as quickly as possible toward ultimate success. These strategies will help you to deal with rejection by: 1) identifying and addressing your feeling and thinking patterns; 2) reviewing your past successes; 3) re-energizing yourself; 4) drawing upon supportive others; 5) defining your specific reasons for getting stuck; 6) brainstorming your options for getting unstuck; 7) making an action plan; and 8) implementing the plan.

Strategy #1: Send Yourself a Different Message

Often, we're unaware that the things we tell ourselves after we're rejected are destructive and blown out of proportion. Make sure that you aren't sending yourself any self-destructive messages, such as:

> *There's no point in following up on that interview. I'm sure they have better candidates.*
> *I hear there are very few jobs in my field for recent college grads. I'm not going to find a job.*

This wait and see thing after interviews is torture. Maybe I'll just stop dealing with organizations after the interview so I can put them out of my mind.

These kinds of messages are powerful, because you can sabotage your best efforts with them. It's only natural to have fears and feel down about your progress. But, the only way you're going to move forward successfully with your job search is to tell yourself more good stuff than bad stuff about how it's going. It's really a matter of not getting in your own way. Be real, but tell yourself a more optimistic story than the day before.

By changing the way we talk to ourselves about rejection, we can recover more quickly and with renewed strength and perspective.

Strategy #2: Create a Success Lifeline.

Another way to deal with rejection is to create a success lifeline. Take a blank 8" by 11" piece of paper and turn it horizontally. Draw a long, horizontal line from the left side of the page to the right side of the page. Place short vertical lines along this horizontal line at different chronological stages from left to right (earliest to latest). Then label the space underneath the horizontal line between each two vertical lines. These blocks of time might be broad, descriptive categories like your preschool years, elementary school years, junior high school years, high school years, etc. Or they can be age-based categories like 1-5 years old, 5-10 years old, etc. It doesn't matter how you label your blocks of time as long as you understand that these blocks will potentially contain success events in your life.

Within each block of time indicate, in any way you choose, a marker of one or more success events. These markers can be symbols, pictures, words, or a combination of these things. These success events can reflect accomplishments which you have been proud of in any aspect of your life—family, hobby, personal growth issue, relationships, education, professional, or other.

Try not to think for too long about your choices before putting them down on paper. When you've placed at least five success events on your lifeline, review them to see if you can discern any patterns or themes among them concerning your definition of success. The connections may be transformations or continuous threads of your definition over time.

Have you selected events in only one or two areas of your life, such as education and work? Are you surprised by your choices? Did they reinforce something you already knew about yourself and your values? Did your memories of success bring back any situations where your success was bouncing back from a rejection or difficult situation? What can you apply from these past experiences to your present one?

Strategy #3: Take Care of Yourself

When you're caught up in the interviewing process, it's easy to forget about your other needs besides a job. Good food, exercise, sleep, hobbies, friends, and other fun activities improve your overall well-being and help you cope with stress. Some fun, inexpensive ways to cope with rejection are the little things that make you happy. For example, when you're feeling blue, get a massage, get back to nature, practice aromatherapy, eat lots of healthy "comfort food" (your childhood favorites), or watch your favorite, funny movie. The less stressed you are, the more inclined you'll be to succeed at your job search. Besides, you deserve it. So give yourself a break and conserve your energy.

Strategy #4: Develop a Support System

Having a support system of people who you can turn to when you're feeling down about your interviewing process can be an invaluable resource for you. Your support system can be as big or as small as you wish. It's a good idea, though, to have more than one supporter in order both to benefit from others' varied experiences and to avoid putting too much pressure on any one relationship. Remembering to select others who you can also support at some point in their job searches will enable you to build a strong support system more comfortably.

Strategy #5: Troubleshoot Your Problems

Just as you need to approach the interviewing process strategically by considering the interviewer's perspective, you need to reflect like an interviewer about what went wrong. Ask yourself: Did I prepare adequately? Did I take control of the interview process? Did I follow-up professionally? Review your debriefing notes (chapter 3, step 19) and the Action Plan Checklists (end of chapters 1, 2, and 3) to make sure that you're effectively using your interviewing techniques. If you discover weaknesses about how you're interviewing, practice improving them.

If you're baffled by what's going wrong, then ask for help Talk to the people in your support system. Start with your inner circle of friends and family members. Then try your college career advisor or independent career counselor as well as uninvolved close professional contacts. All of these people may give you valuable feedback that may help you to regroup and refine your interviewing strategies.

By evaluating your behavior by yourself or with others, you may find that your true problem isn't your ability to implement techniques. Your problem may be something else. For example, you may feel burned out by the interviewing process. Sometimes you're pushing too hard too fast to get your dream job and the intensity of the interviewing process gets to you. A few days away from it can help you feel like you've broken the cycle of failure. You can get back into the interviewing process as a rejuvenated and optimistic candidate.

Another possible reason for getting stuck is that you're really not ready to handle a job interview, or a job, at this point in your life. This lack of readiness doesn't mean that you are a weak or weird person. Many highly intelligent and competent people go through times in their lives when they aren't ready to commit to a first or new job. When they're ready, they more readily secure and enjoy jobs in their fields of interest. In the meantime, though, their interviewing doesn't lead to job offers because interviewers sense their problem. If you're not feeling ready to make the move to a job, that's okay. Give yourself a chance to grow and gain self-confidence.

A third issue may be that you don't know what you really want to do and are just interviewing for random jobs. So when you get in the interview, you discover that the job doesn't fit with your skills, interests, personality, and/or values. You need to have your priorities straight before you can interview for jobs, especially since no job will be a perfect fit. In this case, you need to find out what you want before you get to the interviewing stage, so that you can project enthusiasm and genuine interest to the interviewer.

Finally, it's a tough job market out there. Competition is stiff. So you may find that your qualifications are not as strong as your competitors'. Then you need to focus on developing your skills to make your interviews more successful.

Strategy #6: Brainstorm Your Options

If your interviewing problems aren't solved by a quick fix of practicing your techniques, then consider another approach. Whether you need to bridge maturity, direction, or skill gaps, you can meet your needs by taking a creative approach. Figure out how you can best get what you need through a part-time or temporary job, volunteering or interning, travel, continuing education classes, or a combination of these options. Depending on your financial situation, you may be able to pursue an unpaid internship and a class with a paid, part-time job or temporary work. Or, consider a paid, full-time job that's not in your area of interest or that doesn't even require a college degree but pays the bills while allowing time in the evening or weekends to take a course or do volunteer work. The key is to create a situation that both meets your immediate financial needs and prepares you to ace your next set of interviews for your dream job.

Be aware, though, that these strategies are not foolproof. You may just not be able to get those negative messages out of your mind. Or maybe you don't think you've accomplished anything. Or you aren't meeting your basic needs. Or you don't feel that you have anyone you can turn to for support. Or you decide that all of your debriefing notes show that you're pathetic. Or you feel too paralyzed to try bridging the gaps. When you experience any of these or related things, it's important to realize that sometimes you may have more than the interviewing blues. You may be depressed and benefit from seeking professional help from a licensed therapist.

Remember, almost everyone who braves the interviewing process gets stuck in a rut once in a while. Some days you're feeling great and getting positive results, while others you're down in the dumps and not getting any offers. The good news is that it's possible to get unstuck. Sometimes it just takes more than one strategy and the perspective to know that the rough times will pass.

Strategy #7: Make an Action Plan

Once you've brainstormed your options, your action plan should include your goals and steps to achieve these goals. First write a brief description of your short-term (1-6 months) and long-term (6-12 months) getting unstuck goals. Make sure to frame these goals in realistic, measurable terms, so you'll know when you get there. For example, in 6 months I want to have taken 2 continuing education classes, secured and begun a volunteer position, researched 10 internships, and participated in job search advising through my college career center.

Short-term goals:

_____

_____

_____

_____

Long-term goals:

_____

_____

_____

_____

Then document the steps that you could take to help you achieve your goals. Remember the ideas discussed in the previous strategies as you develop your steps. Also, establish your timetable for taking each of these steps. Be realistic and break what you have to do down into chunks, or small pieces, so that you don't get overwhelmed.

<u>Short-term Action Steps</u>   <u>Time Frames</u>

1.

2.

3.

4.

5.

<u>Long-term Action Steps</u>   <u>Time Frames</u>

1.

2.

3.

4.

5.

Strategy #8: Implement Your Plan

Now it's time to use your plan to take action. Take your plan one step at a time. Find small, meaningful ways to celebrate your accomplishments. Make sure you don't get isolated along the way. Setbacks are inevitable and you'll need support and a sense of humor. So take the process at your own pace, stay flexible, and know that there are concrete ways to ultimately achieve a successful interviewing outcome. The challenge is to make your approach work for you. Your time, money, and effort are valuable commodities. Maximize these resources by taking a strategic approach when you get stuck as well as before, during, and after your interviewing.

EPILOGUE

Maybe you picked up this book the night before an interview and turned straight to a particular step. Or you might have read it from cover to cover to get cut-to-the-chase advice on the whole interviewing process. Whatever you used it for, I hope you remember one key thing: be a strategic self-marketer. That means think like an interviewer about what they need. Then use this mindset to creatively and thoroughly prepare for an interview; assertively equalize your role during the interview; and persistently pursue your interviewer without becoming a pest when you follow-up.

Throughout the interviewing process, you need to sell yourself as the best candidate for the job. It's up to you to show, not just tell, the interviewer that your potential to learn quickly on the job as well as your other skills would add immediate value to their organization.

Now that you know that interviewing doesn't have to feel like an interrogation, or even a major hassle, what are you waiting for? Hang in there and nail that next interview!

ABOUT THE AUTHOR

Marci I. Taub, M.A., is a career counselor in private practice. She specializes in on-site and long-distance career counseling and testing, job search coaching, and educational advising services for clients from teens through early thirties. As an adjunct faculty member of New York University's School of Continuing Education, she develops and teaches courses through the Center for Career, Education, and Life Planning. She is also the co-author of *Job Smart* (The Princeton Review, 1997). Her professional affiliations include memberships in the American Counseling Association and the National Career Development Association.

Prior to entering private practice, she consulted and was employed in human resources with major financial institutions, including Chase Manhattan Bank and Smith Barney. She has also held positions in colleges in New York and New Jersey, advising students on career planning and job search issues. Marci has an M.A. in Counseling from Montclair State University, a Certificate in Adult Career Planning and Development from New York University, and a bachelor's degree from Oberlin College.